Parenting
Gifted
Kids

Parenting
Gifted
Kids

Tips for Raising
Happy
and Successful
Children

James R. Delisle, Ph.D.

Prufrock Press Inc.
Waco, Texas

Library of Congress Cataloging-in-Publication Data

Delisle, James R., 1953-
   Parenting gifted kids : tips for raising happy and successful children
/ by Jim Delisle.
      p. cm.
   Includes bibliographical references.
   ISBN 1-59363-179-0 (pbk.)
      1. Gifted children. 2. Parents of gifted children. 3. Parenting.
   4. Gifted children—Education. 5. Education—Parent participation.
   I. Title.
   HQ773.5.D443 2006
   649'.155—dc22

                                          2005034869

Edited by Lacy Elwood
Layout and cover design by Marjorie Parker

ISBN-13: 978-1-59363-179-6
ISBN-10: 1-59363-179-0

Printed in the United States of America.

At the time of this book's publication, all facts and figures cited are the most current available. All telephone numbers, addresses, and Web site URLs are accurate and active. All
publications, organizations, Web sites, and other resources exist as described in the book,
and all have been verified. The authors and Prufrock Press Inc., make no warranty or
guarantee concerning the information and materials given out by organizations or content found at Web sites, and we are not responsible for any changes that occur after this
book's publication. If you find an error, please contact Prufrock Press Inc. We strongly
recommend to parents, teachers, and other adults that you monitor children's use of the
Internet.

PRUFROCK PRESS INC.
P.O. Box 8813
Waco, Texas 76714–8813
(800) 998-2208
http://www.prufrock.com

Contents

Introduction

The word *tip* has multiple meanings. If you work in the service industry, it means giving (or getting) some extra cash for services delivered well. A tip can also be an end point, a pinnacle, as in the "tip of one's finger." In a book such as this, the word tip would imply to most readers that some type of suggestion would follow—a helpful hint, if you will—on the road to better understanding of that person you live with called "a gifted child."

That would be a good guess, but a wrong one. Here's why: Barnes & Noble and other bookstores are filled with advice books for parents of kids, gifted and otherwise. What these books share in common is common sense, statements such as "let your child live her own life, not yours" or "make it safe for your child to learn through his mistakes." Although this advice isn't bad, it is rather shallow. In fact, the tips in most books on parenting probably don't teach new skills, as much as reinforce the importance of an old one: Nurture your children's independence and creativity so they will reach their "full potential."

Since the existing books on parenting gifted kids answer the basics, I want this book to go in a different direction (I've never been big on reinventing the wheel, in my life or my writing). So, when I use the word tip here, I am not going to provide you with a specific, use-it-tonight suggestion. Instead, the tips I offer will have less to do with actions and more to do with attitude. Case in point: In the previous paragraph, I end with an allusion to children "reaching their full potential." That is a phrase you will not find in this book, or in any of my writing. Why not? Because the term itself—*full potential*—is so vague that it has no meaning or value. I have yet to see a child or adult stand up and proclaim publicly, "I am pleased to announce that I have reached my full potential. Thank you, and good night." Sounds dumb, huh? We fill parenting books with platitudes about "potential" or "risk taking," and then find that our words of solace or advice fall into our children's deaf ear, the one they always point to us when they want to tune us out.

So, here's what to expect in my book: Ten statements that will cause you to reexamine the ways you perceive your child's intelligence and challenges. Each statement will be elaborated upon for clarity and, wherever possible, an instance from the life of a real child or parent with whom I have worked will be included as evidence of the statement's worth. An occasional, usable tip might surface, but my intent is that you will read this book, absorb its messages, and then look at your gifted child through a different set of lenses than you had worn before. What you do with this information will be based on a sound understanding of the hassles, hurdles, and happinesses that make up the life of every gifted child.

Also, don't be surprised if, in reading my book, you get somewhat self-reflective. More often than not, gifted kids come from parents whose intellects are advanced, and reading about the ins-and-outs of childhood giftedness might dredge up memories you didn't even know you had. If that happens . . . enjoy the ride.

Best wishes to you in this learning adventure. I hope you enjoy my book enough that, at its conclusion, you decide to send me that type of tip so common in the service industry. I promise to report every penny to the IRS.

—Jim Delisle

Chapter 1

Understand What Giftedness Is . . . and What It Is Not

At a recent meeting with Jeff's mom and several of his teachers, I was amazed that the majority of the people sitting around the conference table were discussing the legitimacy of this boy's giftedness. At 14 years old, Jeff already had quite a school history, which, truth be told, fizzled more than it sparkled. With an IQ of 145, but grades of D's and F's, Jeff was a walking frustration to most adults. The teachers' conversation went something like this:

"You know, if Jeff was really gifted, he'd show it once in a while."

"Yes, and his homework is never done . . . "

" . . . And let's not even talk about his organizational skills! You know, the ones he doesn't have?"

I could tell that Jeff's mom wanted to interrupt and offer a different perspective—the one that noticed Jeff could read a 350-page historical novel in 2 days; or that he started his school career at age 5 with panache, vigor, and an urge to

1

learn; or that Jeff's vocabulary and thinking processes were more advanced than most adults, including some of his teachers. Yet, she stayed mute. Why? She had expressed such realities before, only to be told the educational equivalent of Jeff's need to "shape-up or ship out."

"Mrs. Rogers," the school counselor concluded, "I believe it is in Jeff's best interests to be moved out of the honors level classes. Perhaps he is too stressed by their rigor."

" . . . Or not?" I added, daring to ask just a single question, "When does Jeff excel?"

This came as a jolt to many of Jeff's teachers. They had come to see this young man as lazy, disheveled, and obstinate, yet the few times Jeff did shine were when he was allowed to do projects of personal interest, or open-ended assignments with multiple right answers, or no right answers at all. He loved logic puzzles, and finished them quickly. He contributed to debates about politics or ecology or justice with a sense of sophistication and insight seldom observed in overzealous young teens who often only boast opinions without regard for the facts. In my mind, there was no doubting Jeff's giftedness. He simply chose not to display it in school activities that required him to do little more than regurgitate facts he had already learned years before. Jeff's teachers may have been disappointed in him, but the reverse was also true—Jeff was disappointed in them.

Perhaps this scenario is familiar to you, as Jeff may be a prototype for your own gifted sons or daughters who play by their own rules, not the school's. Or, you may be a parent who is sitting back thinking, "I guess I'm lucky that my child has always prized achievement." Whatever the case may be, know this: Giftedness should not—indeed, *must* not—be linked to achievement in order to be a legitimate entity. Calling Jeff (or anyone) gifted only when they can prove it by jumping through the artificial achievement hoops we place before them is equivalent to saying that a disease can only exist if its symptoms are obvious and visible.

As a parent, you may believe this already, as you have an asset that most schoolteachers do not—you knew your child from the start. Teachers, even the ones who work with our kids for several years, still see only a snapshot of their full selves; a place-in-time moment that may or may not be an accurate depiction of the fullness of the child's being. It is your long-range opinion that matters most, and the key to getting others to see the giftedness in your child as being an inherent quality rather than a report card filled with A's is knowing, first and foremost, that your impressions are accurate.

> As a parent ... you have an asset that most schoolteachers do not—you knew your child from the start

Speaking of First Impressions ...

When I entered the realm of gifted child education in 1978, I was a doctoral student seeking answers. I didn't realize how lucky I was to become, for within a year, I met two women whose views on giftedness are the most profound and legitimate our field has ever produced. Both of them gave me answers to the issue of giftedness that have stayed with me to this day. You need to know about them, too.

The first is a woman I met only through her work, Leta S. Hollingworth. Hollingworth died in 1939, yet her work spoke to me in such a way that whenever I opened one of her books, I felt like we were sitting in a coffeeshop in overstuffed chairs with bad upholstery; I, taking notes and Leta, just talking. A school psychologist by trade, Hollingworth was teaching a course at Columbia University in 1916 on the psychology of "mentally deficient children" (her phrase). Using the newly minted Stanford-Binet IQ test, Hollingworth wanted her students to see a contrast between children who scored at the lower limits of the test and one child who scored much higher. She arranged to test an 8-year-old boy called Child E, "who exhausted the scale without being fully measured by it, achieving an IQ of *at least* 187" (Hollingworth, 1942, p. xii). From this moment on, Hollingworth was hooked, as she wrote,

> I had tested thousands of incompetent persons, a majority of them children . . . this thoroughgoing experience of the negative aspects of intelligence rendered the performance of E even more impressive to me than it would otherwise have been. I perceived the clear and flawless working of his mind against a contrasting background of thousands of dull and foolish minds. It was an unforgettable observation. (p. xii)

Hollingworth did groundbreaking work in establishing the field of giftedness as a legitimate entity. In addition to being a psychologist and author, she also taught highly gifted children in a program she developed for the New York City public school system. In every regard, she came to see giftedness as a quality that can be measured at a young age, and that this quality, this giftedness, is a lifelong phenomenon that may or may not show itself in high achievement. A passage from her book, *Children Above 180 IQ, Stanford-Binet*, published posthumously in 1942, contains many passages that, sadly, are as true today as they were then:

> This element in our juvenile population, so significant and so rarely found, passes unrecognized at present through the public schools. We have not even commenced to evolve an education suitable

for a child who at 9 or 10 years of age is able to think on a college level. The idea that such children exist at all is even laughed to scorn by teachers and principals who have a quarter of a century of "experience" behind them. These children have no way of making themselves known. They become known only to those educators who "believe in" mental tests. (1942, p. 320)

If the true definition of a visionary is someone whose work is even more legitimate in the generations that follow its creation, then Leta S. Hollingworth fits the bill. A champion of gifted children as people that must be acknowledged and accommodated, Hollingworth remains a beacon of hope for today's gifted children, and those who care about them.

The other woman whom I met during my first year in studying gifted children was Annemarie Roeper. And, unlike Hollingworth, Annemarie entered my life in the real sense, and our friendship is among my most cherished possessions.

Annemarie has worked with gifted children and their families since the 1940s, when she and her husband, George, opened a school in southeastern Michigan based on a philosophy of global interdependence and personal, emotional well-being. The school had a rich foundation, as Annemarie's parents ran a boarding school in Germany with similar emphases. Yes, academic achievement was prized, but it had to be considered as only one part of a child's education; art, culture, and a firm understanding of the importance of each person's existence were the other colors on the palette of life that were essential if one were to become truly educated, truly human. Beginning humbly as a nursery school housed in the top floor of their home, The Roeper School now boasts an enrollment of more than 600 gifted and creative children from nursery school through 12th grade. As two parents said about their child's experiences at Roeper, "My son can write a paper with 35 footnotes, and he also knows that everybody deserves his respect," and "There's no division between jocks and intellectuals. It's assumed everybody has a body and a mind" (Delisle, 2000, p. 41).

The contributions made by George and Annemarie Roeper concerning the appropriate education of gifted, young minds could fill volumes, yet the most important piece of the "gifted puzzle" (from my admittedly biased perch), was a simple conception of giftedness given by Annemarie: "Giftedness is a greater awareness, a greater sensitivity, and a greater ability to understand and transform perceptions into intellectual and emotional experiences" (Roeper, 2000, p. 33).

Go ahead—think of the gifted child or adult who brought you to open this book in the first place. Now, reread Annemarie's conception of giftedness. I'd bet a large wager that her conception of giftedness is more closely aligned to what you see in the gifted individual(s) in your life than any definition pointing to a particular IQ number or achievement test percentile. Essentially, gifted people come to our attention first and foremost because of the sophisticated ways they perceive the world around them. True, their vocabularies may arrive early and large, and their abilities to connect seemingly disparate concepts seem ingrained from an early age, but it is their overall awareness of and sensitivity to the people and surroundings that inhabit their lives that distinguish them from their age peers. And this, my friends, is giftedness.

Case in point: In describing the gifted child in her life, one mom said this in response to the question "What is giftedness?":

Their minds are black holes, endless pits that you just keep pouring information into as they beg for more. Life for them is an existential dichotomy—simultaneously too much and never enough. Time is not a concept they acknowledge, just an unnecessary intrusion into their world of fascination. It's true they have infinite potential . . . but being eminently aware of the infinity concept, they are often completely overwhelmed with the multitude of choices and interests that lay before them. They challenge everyone around them—parent, teacher or friend— to be the very best they can be. If you're really lucky (and it doesn't kill you), you get to be all three. (Personal communication, November 11, 1999)

Upon her retirement as headmistress of the Roeper School in 1983, Annemarie and George moved to California, where Annemarie developed the Annemarie Roeper Model of Qualitative Assessment (QA). During this assessment process, Annemarie interviews parents of a gifted child and the gifted child him- or herself, and then follows this up with a final discussion with the parents in which recommendations for schools and family interaction are offered. The core of this QA is the interview with the child, which may last up to 90 minutes. As expressed by Annemarie:

The goal is not for children to show how much they know or how bright they are, but who they are. The information presents itself in a pure form, almost like a byproduct. This is sacred information and must never be misused . . . The child may keep a distance, seem to be oblivious of the evaluator, or get close, touch, talk trustingly, excitedly, or be eager to share. The secret is to further the flow of expression, when needed, without changing it. (Roeper, 2004, p. 33)

And, at the session's conclusion . . .

> It is amazing for me to see how reluctant the children usually are to leave, even though I am old, cannot hear well, cannot get down on the floor with them, and do not have the latest toys. It is because they feel understood, recognized and accepted. (Roeper, 2004, p. 33)

In determining what giftedness "looks like," it would serve us well to consider the contributions of Leta Hollingworth and Annemarie Roeper. Both pioneers, they have established giftedness as an entity that can be measured best through observation and the careful, tender analysis of the child's abilities to perceive the world from a view that is both sophisticated and complex.

Reality Sets In

As you might imagine, the views of giftedness expressed above are not the ones used by school districts or departments of education in qualifying children for gifted program services. Far from it. Instead, the "definitions" of giftedness they use are often little more than mathematical formulae that result in two piles of kids—the "ins" and the "outs."

The small part of me that is realistic understands the reasoning behind this process. Indeed, it would be difficult to conduct a qualitative assessment similar to Roeper's on every child brought to the attention of school personnel as possibly being gifted. Time and cost prohibitive, this procedure is relinquished in favor of group test scores on aptitude and achievement tests.

To be fair, this is not a bad place to begin; test scores can tell us which children are excelling in relation to their agemates. The problem comes when the test scores become the *only* way for a child to gain access to gifted program services. As we know, some children do not test well, whether due to nervousness, a language or cultural difference, or because the child would rather make an intricate design on the bubble sheet than answer "stupid questions on a stupid test." So, if we stop at the test scores, we may be doing two bad things: not identifying gifted kids who deserve to be noticed, and overidentifying high achievers as gifted when they are little more than . . . well, high achievers.

Here is what should happen: Once test scores are collected, school personnel should pass around to the teachers the list of students who scored in the top 5% of each grade level, on aptitude (IQ), achievement, or both. Then, ask one simple question, "Who is not on this list who deserves closer examination?" Even if only a few names are suggested, these children can then be examined with a more informal procedure, perhaps one that approximates Roeper's QA, or involves an examination of the child's body of work in or outside of school. Flawless? Hardly, yet this simple procedure could yield a bounty of gifted kids who may not qualify for the label by the more typical, numeric procedures.

If all else fails, and your child's school is reluctant (or worse) to look beyond the test scores, you may need to resort to an individual intellectual assessment conducted by the school's psychologist or a psychologist in private practice. This can be expensive, in terms of dollars and time, yet it is often worth the effort to have this test completed. Why? Because few school districts will discount the evaluation of a professional who is licensed to administer and interpret a noted IQ test like the Stanford-Binet or the Wechsler Intelligence Scale for Children (WISC).

Avoid at All Costs

There is one conception of giftedness some schools have selected to use that will put your child at a decided disadvantage. Developed by Joseph Renzulli in 1978, the so-called Three-Ring conception of giftedness relies on the following qualities to be identified: above-average intelligence (no problem there), creativity (and how is this measured?), and task commitment (sustained efforts on all things academic). However, these qualities alone are not sufficient to be identified as gifted; according to Renzulli, the child *must* show that he or she is applying these attributes in a visible way, in a tangible product. If not, the gifted door is shut to him or her. Thus, a child of 7 who asks questions about life and death and God would not be considered gifted, unless he chose to put together some type of project—a diorama of the universe, perhaps? And, a ninth grader with a 140 IQ would not be considered gifted unless she manufactured some type of product to prove how smart she is. Her keen insights into the human condition would not suffice to qualify her as gifted. And kids who underachieve in school? Forgetaboutit. Using Renzulli's conception of giftedness, an "underachieving gifted child" is a contradiction of terms.

Based solely on the work of grown-ups who have achieved eminence due to their adult accomplishments, this view of giftedness has no place in the world of children.

Just a Word on Leveling

Before I began my career in working with and for gifted children, my area of specialty was mental retardation. I taught children who were called, at the time, "educable mentally retarded." These kids had some skills in language, reading, and comprehending social interactions. They learned slowly, yet they were often able to function in society with varying levels of assistance. In the classroom next to mine was a group of children who were called "trainable mentally retarded." Seldom could these children be left unattended, as their levels of skill and logic were very low. Often, their education consisted of learning to dress or feed themselves, and language, if present at all, consisted of words, not sentences. Obviously, children in these two classrooms had very different learning needs, and our curriculum adjusted for these individual idiosyncrasies.

When I entered the field of gifted child education, I assumed the same distinction would apply. However, I would come to know children who were "gifted" and others who were, well . . . "super gifted." I soon learned that few school districts take the time to differentiate between levels of giftedness the same way they do for children with disabilities. Instead, all the gifted kids were clustered under one label, often receiving the same services in the same classroom. Yet, even if IQ alone were used to identify these children, the range of scores might be from 130–180+, which is a far greater range of IQ then I ever dealt with in my class for children who were mentally retarded.

Although it is hard to generalize about the needs of children I have not met, my experiences with gifted children lead me to state the following:

- Children with IQs in the 130–140 range can often be accommodated in regular classrooms where teachers adjust the curriculum to meet their advanced abilities. Social and emotional difficulties are uncommon, as there is a large enough pool of children with similar abilities that legitimate friendships can be formed.

- Children with IQ's in the 140–160 range can seldom be accommodated sufficiently in an educational environment that merely "stretches" or enriches the curriculum. Intensive modification of curriculum, including grade skipping, needs to be considered as viable. Too, agemates may offer little social sustenance, as these children will prefer—and need—the company of older, intelligent children and/or adults.

- Children with IQs above 160 have academic and intellectual needs that are so unique that typical school resources will be unable to provide fully for their education. For these rare children, a team of professionals (including a teacher, gifted expert, parents, and a psychologist) will need to be convened, much as a similar team would be gathered for a child with severe learning difficulties. Intellectually, socially, and emotionally, these profoundly gifted children are more at risk than others if their level of giftedness is not addressed directly.

In recent years, more information and resources have become available for highly gifted children and their parents (see Appendix A: Resources for Parents). Just know this: Because giftedness varies in both depth and range, your advocacy efforts on behalf of your child will need to take into account both of these realities. If "one-size-fits-all" isn't true in shoes, shirts, or pantyhose, then it is equally unrealistic to believe that a single gifted program can serve the needs of its many unique members.

Talking the Talk

A wise 14-year-old girl, highly gifted and highly verbal, once asked me the following questions: "Have you watched adults squirm, and listened to their responses when you ask them if they're gifted? What does this say about how they define giftedness, and what messages does this send to people, especially kids, about giftedness being OK?"

Even though most parents see giftedness as a positive attribute, they are often reluctant to talk openly about the term and its implications with their children. Fearing their gifted children will become "elitist" or "big-headed" if the term is discussed, parents downplay the term and advise their gifted children to do the same, "so that other kids don't feel bad."

> By not discussing giftedness, or by telling your gifted child to avoid mention of it around others, you are sending a confusing, mixed message—be proud of your abilities, but don't let anyone know you have them.

Yeah . . . just like you'd be quiet about it if your child happened to be a star athlete!

By not discussing giftedness, or by telling your gifted child to avoid mention of it around others, you are sending a confusing, mixed message—be proud of your abilities, but don't let anyone know that you have them.

An attitude of humility regarding one's advanced abilities is understandable, but it can go too far. When it gets to the point that a gifted child appears downright embarrassed to say that he is in a gifted program, or that he has skipped a grade because of his strong academic abilities, the child is not being humble, but dishonest. So are you, if you promote such behavior.

When your child is identified as gifted, take time to sit down with him or her and explain *in your own words* what you think this term means. Give your child some cues that you picked up at an early age ("You know, Shawna, I remember you were reading cereal boxes and road signs when you were not even 2 years old."), and let them know that just because they may learn quicker than other kids, that doesn't imply an inherent superiority as a human being. Your child might be *better at* many things than the kid next door, but that does not mean that they are *better than* that child in any way. Next, ask your gifted children if they ever noticed that they can do things or understand things that many kids their age do not yet get. And, ask them if they often find that they like talking or playing with older kids or adults, as the level of understanding or camaraderie in these mixed-age groupings just seems like a comfortable, intellectual fit. If they say they do like the company of elders, tell them that this is common among gifted kids.

Next, be ready for the inevitable question, "Mom (Dad) . . . were you gifted?" First, you will chuckle, as kids always ask this question in the past tense, as if your own giftedness as a parent somehow went away or awry in the adult years. Follow your guffaw with a genuine answer that doesn't fall back to the standard nonresponse of "We didn't have gifted programs when I was in school." Your children are not asking whether you were placed in gifted classes. They are asking, "Are you one of me?" Be honest with a genuine "yes" or "no," as it can open the door up to a conversation about a word that needs to be taken out of the closet and shaken from its musty, stale image: *gifted*.

One last thing: When your child comes home with the tears flowing after a bad day at school (it'll happen) because someone made fun of her for getting a low grade on some meaningless test, she'll probably ask you this, "Why do I have to be gifted? Why can't I just be normal like everyone else?" You need to be prepared. The word *normal* is a loaded word, as its opposite, *abnormal*, is something few of us aspire to be. Contrasting the terms *gifted* and *normal* implies that giftedness is an aberration, a flaw, something to be avoided. Hear your child out, and then ask her to sub-stitute only one word—change *normal* to *typical*. The plaintive cry of "Why can't I be typical?" sounds just a bit less harsh than "normal," doesn't it? With a little cajoling and a dose of hot cocoa, you might even get into a discussion of how giftedness is often determined by a child's doing things in advance of when most other kids do. It may be atypical to know your alphabet by 18 months, but because all kids learn the alphabet in their own time, there's nothing abnormal about that, is there?

In the next chapter, we'll take a closer look at that distinction between *better at* and *better than*, especially as it might impact social relationships. For now, though, I leave you with some wise words that might spur even more discussion with your children about the meaning of this often misunderstood term, *gifted*.

Gifted Children Speak Out

"I have always felt different somehow—misplaced or misborn. I remember being perplexed and vaguely disappointed on the first day of school because it seemed so simplistic. I wondered about the competency and qualifications of my teacher. In the middle of fourth grade, I was pulled from my classroom and sent to a closet with a teacher and two other students. It was a month or so before I realized I had been *identified* as gifted and was now receiving *enrichment*. No one ever told me."

—Boy, age 14

"When I was first placed in the gifted program, nobody explained to me what that meant. So, when people would ask me and I couldn't tell them, they would say that I should know because I was smarter than they were."

—Girl, age 13

"No one ever told us what exactly 'gifted' means—or what 'ungifted' means. It could mean that I can ace tests, but I still can't write a decent essay for beans. But an 'ungifted' kid I know can write like an author but flunks tests because he freezes. So, which of us is 'gifted' and which is 'ungifted?'"

—Boy, age 14

Chapter 2

Know the Distinction Between "Better At" and "Better Than"

I n my first teaching job in northern New Hampshire, there were only three conditions under which we would not have outdoor recess—if the temperature was lower than negative 10 degrees, if there was a moose in the schoolyard, or if the town drunk, Mr. Shibley, was on the swings again. Barring these circumstances . . . out we went! And, it was during one of my daily recess duties that I first came to learn of the plight of gifted children when it comes to honest communication.

Two first-grade boys were having a fight. No blood or weapons were involved, just a lot of screaming and flailing of little arms that never hit the intended targets of each other. As I calmed the boys down, one of the young combatants hurled off some verbal insults to his opponent, "I hate you, you're stupid, you're a pig." Not to be outshouted, the other boy—who I knew from reputation to be very bright—spouted off the ultimate degradation, "I might be a pig, but you're a Neanderthal!"

The world stopped for a moment, as the young audience who had gathered looked at one another with wrinkled noses and sighed a collective "Huh?" Imagine—being so smart that even your insults are misunderstood.

Don't get me wrong, I'm not in favor of anything that hints of an insult or put-down, yet I do suspect that when such negative verbiage is spewed, the spewer intends for the spewee to comprehend it. After all, how can we call it communication if the message sent is never truly received?

The distinction between *better at* and *better than* involves many issues that serve gifted children well, if they understand what they are. Too often called *nerd*, *geek*, *smarty pants*, *brainiac*, or worse, gifted kids need to know that the source of these insults is one of two things—envy or ignorance. However, when a gifted kid tries to defend himself from name calling by telling his accuser, "You're only saying that because you're jealous of my abilities," or "If you weren't so stupid you'd get what I'm saying," well, it doesn't improve the situation even an iota.

Let's delve into this fine-line distinction by returning to the work of someone you've already met, Leta Hollingworth.

On Suffering Fools Gladly

A lesson which many gifted persons never learn as long as they live is that human beings in general are inherently very different from themselves in thought, in action, in general intention, and in interests. Many a reformer has died at the hands of a mob which he was trying to improve in the belief that other human beings can and should enjoy what he enjoys. This is one of the most painful and difficult lessons that each gifted child must learn, if personal development is to proceed successfully. It is more necessary that this be learned than that any school subject be mastered. (Hollingworth, 1942, pp. 259–260)

The wisdom of Hollingworth's statements transcends time once again. Because no child rises after a full night's sleep, stretches to awaken tired muscles and brain cells, and states openly, "Gee . . . I wonder who I can get to hate me today at school," it is obvious that person-to-person communication is valued. No one seeks to be isolated or void of friendships and lunchtime buddies, but more than occasionally, gifted children find themselves spending time alone, at least intellectually. Barely keeping their heads above water in discussing topics of little interest to them, gifted kids often wonder, "Isn't there someone like *me* out there?"

It's at this point that you, as a parent, need to intervene and present two realities to your gifted child—the idea of suffering fools gladly, and, simultaneously, the distinction between agemates and peers.

First, let's review *suffering fools gladly* through a fairly common example. A bunch of 5-year-olds get together and decide to play a game. One of them, your gifted daughter, can't wait to play; games have rules, people take turns, and there is a goal to achieve, like being the first player to enter Candy Land. Before the game even starts, though, there are squabbles—two kids fight over who gets the blue marker, no one seems to get that all people play first before your turn comes around again—indeed, the idea of taking turns just seems foreign to your daughter's playmates. So, she responds by taking charge, assigning roles, and saying things like "It's not your turn yet." The other kids look at her as the spoilsport, saying she is no fun, and a bad friend. In essence, your daughter's intellect and maturity cause her to define *fun* differently than do most 5-year-olds. In the end, the other kids walk away, leaving your daughter sad, disillusioned, and confused.

Fast-forward 10 years, to that level of hell Dante forgot to write about in *The Inferno*—ninth grade. Your gifted son is excited that the enthusiastic student teacher has selected *Romeo and Juliet* as the class reading assignment. It won't be a watered down version translated into modern English, it will be the original play—just as Shakespeare wrote it. There will even be a chance to act out some of the scenes, with classmates playing the roles of the main characters. Then it happens: Between some kids saying, "This stuff makes no sense," to others giggling over the thought that a boy and girl might touch hands—or kiss!—if they play their roles as written, the serious intent of the student teacher is DOA. Your son comes home, slams his books on the kitchen table and shouts (as if it's your fault . . .), "Why can't these kids GROW UP? I'm SICK of them!"

These two scenes, if they occur repeatedly throughout your gifted child's life, could cause her to resent the people with whom she spends much of her day—her classmates. In a valiant effort to get other children to comprehend and appreciate the bigger picture, your child becomes the know-it-all, the gifted geek who only wants things her way. No longer willing to agonize silently, the gifted child lashes out—somewhere, sometime—or even worse, represses these feelings, causing a turmoil that cripples her insides.

That's why the notion of suffering fools gladly needs to be raised as soon as you witness an incident like the ones above. Tell your child the truth: "The kids who don't want to play games by the rules or have no idea of the relevance of Shakespeare *are* immature, by comparison to you. However, they are not being immature on purpose. Right now, this is simply who they are." Such a statement may not bring a lot of solace to your child, but it presents him with a stark reality that he may, indeed, encounter into adulthood—age and maturity are sometimes poles apart. Let your child know, too, that trying to convince classmates (or, in the future, colleagues) that they are acting more like their hat sizes than their ages will not be met with a lot of acceptance, for just as you don't get your classmates . . . they just don't get you. Hollingworth's advice? She said it above, if you try to reform the mob, you may be the one who is martyred.

So, what to do? Here's where you bring out the heavy social artillery—reviewing the distinction between agemates and peers. Simply put, an agemate is someone who was born in the same year as you. You may or may not have a lot in common other than the proximity of your birthday, but the assumption is that you are peers because of your similarity in chronology. Schools are established around the agemate concept, as the vast majority of kids start kindergarten at age 5 and graduate high school at 18. In those intervening 13 years (especially in elementary school), it's unusual for kids of mixed ages to be together in the same classroom for an extended period. Why? It is assumed that the people you have the most in common with are your agemates, so there is no need to stray to another grade level to find common social or intellectual ground.

A peer, by contrast, is someone who shares your passions, your humor, and your drive. You can talk for hours about anything—or nothing at all—and there is a sense of comfort present that you can say what you want, even using that big vocabulary that makes your agemates twitch their noses in confusion. How old you are is either irrelevant or of minor importance, and is generally only raised as an issue by someone who does not understand that soulmates don't factor in age as a variable for friendship.

... gifted children often prefer the company of adults or older children. The reason is obvious: They don't need to explain who they are or how they know what they know.

It is common knowledge that gifted children often prefer the company of adults or older children. The reason is obvious: They don't need to explain who they are or how they know what they know. Accepted as bright, competent individuals, the stigma of being smart is not a stigma at all.

Ironically, this agemate/peer distinction seems both understood and accepted once K–12 schooling is complete. Once in college or employed, people of all ages study, work, and play together, and I have yet to see a party invitation for adults include the notation, "Sorry, if you are younger than 25 or older than 32, please pass along this invitation to someone who is within that age bracket." Let your gifted child know this, too: As years pass, their specific chronological age will play less and less a factor in socialization. This is not to say that they won't meet some grownups who remain the dolts they were in high school, but it does open up the social arena to a whole batch of people who may have been off limits during the K–12 years.

There is, though, one group of agemates who can also play the roles as peers: other gifted children. Time and again, you will hear gifted children say that they appreciate their advanced classes for two reasons—the education they are receiving and the people who surround them in learning it. Indeed, I would argue that the greatest benefit of gifted programming is not the high-level content the students study, it is the benefit of learning alongside "like minds." You know, those kids who, in a schoolyard fight among first graders, would understand the word Neanderthal . . . and might even know its correct pronunciation.

Oh! The Silly Things We Do!

One of the more accurate depictions of a gifted child in the media is Malcolm from the TV show *Malcolm in the Middle*. The third oldest of four boys (so how can he be "in the middle"?), Malcolm's IQ of 165 is noted as he is entering adolescence, and it is not an asset he welcomes. Here's why: On the day Malcolm is to leave his regular classroom to begin work with the gifted teacher, his classroom teacher brings Malcolm up to the front of the room for a congratulatory sendoff. With Malcolm facing his classmates, his well-meaning teacher mentions how smart Malcolm is and just how proud the whole class should be for him. "He doesn't look any different," the teacher explains, "but Malcolm IS different . . . in his brain." Of course, the class bully cannot wait for lunch recess, when he intends to put Malcolm's brain on display in a far more visceral way (Boomer, 2000).

Why do otherwise smart adults do such things? In noting an able child's differences in front of agemates, or in mentioning how surprised we are when a gifted child does something silly or wrong ("I expected more common sense from a smart girl like you!"), we are actually setting the scene for social trouble. Terms like *suck up*, *teacher's pet*, or the revolting imagery of *brown noser*, don't even begin to describe the feelings of loneliness some gifted children feel when they are pinpointed as paragons of perfect behavior. Here are just some of the silly ways adults put gifted students on edge . . . and at risk for social isolation:

- *Forgetting that they are children first and gifted second.* Often, gifted children act more responsibly than other kids their age. They remember their school assignments and household chores, and if we ask them to remind us of an important date, deadline, or appointment, they'll often do so. Conversations with adults are likely to be appropriate, and the use of logic over tantrums is generally how conflicts at school or in the family are resolved. And then, there are the days when *none* of these things is true and you begin to wonder if that gifted child you saw yesterday had an overnight lobotomy. Scratching your head, you say to yourself, "I thought he was smarter than this." The thing is, kids are supposed to be immature, selfish, forgetful, and less concerned about tomorrow than today. That's their job. Just because gifted children tend to act this way less often than others their age does not mean we should chide them when they do act in ways that would not raise eyebrows if they were not so smart.

> The thing is, kids are supposed to be immature, selfish, forgetful, and less concerned about tomorrow than today. That's their job. Just because gifted children tend to act this way less often than others their age does not mean we should chide them when they do act in ways that would not raise eyebrows if they were not so smart.

- *Putting the gifted child on display for other adults.* I can hear it now, "Honey, when company comes over tonight, will you play your violin for them? I'm sure they'd love to hear you!" Through gritted teeth, your child may comply grudgingly or may decide to play in such an off-key way that the cat seeks cover, your company squirms as if sitting on rocks—and your child is freed from ever having to perform again in the living room.

With the exception of young children and kids with ego problems, very few others like to be put on display in an artificial environment. No problem if your company decides to go to the school orchestra concert with you—hey, in that case, they know what they're getting into—but performing at home when the child's preference would be to greet your company politely and then exit for a round of reading or video games is not a way to build pride. It is, for you, a way to boast.

- *Putting the gifted child on display in front of other kids.* Again, if it's a band concert, a soccer match, a spelling bee, or a stage production of *Our Town,* observers expect to be wowed. Kids and adults alike realize that in a competitive event or in a culminating show based on much practice, the best that you can be is the best! However, if a teacher singles out a student in class by saying "There was only one A on Friday's test, can anyone guess who got it?" or "I wish *all* of you would follow Felipe's lead and read books that are longer than 100 pages," the comment itself may be having the exact opposite of the effect you intend. For smart kids, it doesn't take them long to realize that to avoid this unwanted adulation in front of classmates, all they have to do is give wrong answers on purpose, pick shorter books from the library, or leave their hands down in class even when they know the right answer to the teacher's question. Game playing? You bet. But, in the world of social survival, it's a game worth winning if you are a gifted kid who doesn't want to stand out at the cost of social acceptance.

- *Expecting gifted children to be natural leaders.* Some gifted children love the limelight and seek it out whenever and however they can. Extroverted by nature, these confident children have Teflon personalities that ward off criticisms from agemates. Then there are those gifted children who are quieter, more reserved, less prone to seek recognition than to amble through life undetected, seldom drawing attention to themselves or their accomplishments. Neither of these types of children is right or wrong, good or bad—the differences are simply innate, a quirk in individual personalities that makes the entire human race so interesting. However, there is a myth that pervades the gifted community: That gifted children are our future leaders and, as such, they should start preparing for these unchosen roles right now. Indeed, gifted programs are sometimes defended by zealots who proclaim that if we don't address the needs of gifted kids today, we are tossing aside tomorrow's changemakers by ignoring them.

Well, not exactly. Although many of our gifted children will grow to become tomorrow's societal mucky-mucks, some of them won't. Further, there will be children who have never been identified as gifted who will outshine early predictions and rise to levels of prominence few teachers would have predicted. We just don't know.

However, to state unequivocally that gifted students will grow to become our future leaders is an insult to one group (those nongifted kids who may grow up to surprise us with their talents) and a source of intense, unwanted pressure on those young people who wear the gifted tag. Too, if you are seeking one more way to make gifted children stand out in an uncomfortable way from others in their school, simply call them tomorrow's leaders while leaving other kids coping with the belief that they will, by default, rise only to the level of our low expectations.

Loneliness and Being Alone: A Fine-Line Distinction

Dr. Dorothy Sisk, former executive director of the federal Office of Gifted and Talented and a remarkable teacher of gifted children, spoke of coming to appreciate a gifted child's personal style:

> I began teaching a "cluster group" of gifted young-sters and when I look back on it, *those* gifted children taught *me*. Many of the strategies I have used over the years I used because of their needs. A story that comes to mind: In those days, we had playground duty and I remember standing out on the field and Dale—who was probably my high-est gifted kid, a brilliant, brilliant child—was way off by himself by the fence. So I asked Ralph to go see what was wrong with Dale. As I watched him run over to Dale, and then return quickly, Ralph said, "Dale's OK—he's just thinking." From that encounter I internalized the idea that gifted kids sometimes need to be alone. Sometimes they just need to think. Nobody taught me that—or, I guess Dale did. (Delisle, 2000, p. 147–148)

One of any parent's greatest fears—whether or not their child is gifted—is that he or she will be lonely, friendless, and isolated from the social milieu that turns loners into isolates. The entire world is a social fabric of interactions with others, and if we find our children are left out of the weave, we fear for them, and rightly so.

For reasons already explained in this chapter, gifted children may appear to be more at risk for being able to participate joyously in social times. However, be reassured that gifted children seek the same type of social comforts others enjoy and they seldom make active attempts to be antisocial. Still, being alert to Hollingworth's (1942) wise assertion that isolation is the "refuge of genius, not its goal," parents of gifted children do want to be vigilant of their child's interactions, or lack thereof, with classmates, age-mates, and peers. But, as discovered by Dorothy Sisk, these interactions might be accompanied by something cloyingly called *alone time*, an essential element in the life of many a gifted individual.

> **Being alone means that you value your mind enough that you would like it to accompany you occasionally on an otherwise solo mission into better understanding yourself and the world.**

There is a difference between being lonely and simply being alone. Being lonely hurts, and it is a state often accompanied by sadness, resignation, or lethargy. Being alone means that you value your mind enough that you would like it to accompany you occasionally on an otherwise solo mission into better understanding yourself and the world. Through generations of work with gifted individuals, it has been found that this alone time is often a necessary and valuable adjunct to one's more social interactions. A mind whirring with ideas, insights, and possibilities sometimes needs time to churn these things together in a cauldron of quiet reflection. This isolation is not to be dismissed as trivial, for as Dorothy Sisk discovered with Dale, it was his time to ponder the wonders of the universe, or to simply relax his ever-active brain for a few moments of peaceful reflection.

In closing, a story: I was working with a group of 20 highly gifted children at a weekend retreat for them and their parents at a tucked away piece of heaven in the Sierra Nevada. The children did not know each other before this weekend, and many of them, even at the tender ages of 4–10, had been burned by unfulfilling contacts with kids their own ages. Then, the activities began, discussions ensued, sandcastles were constructed, and meals were shared. At the Sunday evening closing dinner, a 10-year-old boy had a personal message to leave with the assembled group: "I wasn't really sure I wanted to come here for this," Anthony explained, "but this has been the best weekend of my life."

Anthony, surrounded by others like himself in terms of interests and intellectual sophistication, found something in this gifted group that he had never found before—peers aplenty.

Gifted Children Speak Out

"My neighbor has been my friend since kindergarten, but now he seems to be shying away from me. Like, if I were to correct him he'd be like, 'You're too smart' or 'You're too preppy.' It hurts, especially because he has been my best friend for so many years."

—Girl, age 13

"Kids in my school are just like crabs in a bucket. They pull each other right back down."

—Boy, age 14

"We worry about lots of world problems our classmates know nothing about, making it harder to relate to them."

—Boy, age 13

"It's fun being smart in the beginning, but people always ask you for help, which is OK, but I need to get my stuff done, too. I just wish people would understand that I'm not any different than the average teenager outside of thought processes. I still have little experience in the world, same as them."

—Girl, age 15

Chapter 3

Stop Paying Interest on a Bill You Never Owed

L ife is filled with false alarms. Thinking you left the front door open or the iron plugged in, you rush home to find that everything is locked up and turned off. Or, your 7-year-old runs in screaming, "Mom! Mom! Come here! Quick!" In a frenzy of motion, you rush to aid your child who excitedly shows you the blue-hatched shell of a robin's egg she found in the backyard. "Isn't it pretty?" your child beams, while you double-check your supply of antacids.

There are so many real sources of fear and foreboding in our world, that it is pointless to manufacture any more, yet we do it all the time. The same is true when it comes to personality traits possessed by many gifted people. What should be seen as pieces of wonder, excitement, imagination, and insight are too often interpreted as weirdness, eccentricity, illogic, and illusionary realities. We take the qualities that cause a gifted person to see the world from a slightly different vantage than most, and we try to homogenize them into the more common, acceptable views of existence. Thus, fuchsia fades to pink. Goldenrod melts to yellow. Sapphire becomes dark blue.

Intensities in your gifted child can take many forms, but instead of giving you a technical definition, let's simply consider what they look like in your home:

- Your son's teacher sends you a note that reads, "Although I love Joey's enthusiasm, he must stop shouting out his answers in class. Also, please talk to him about the incessant tapping of his pencil, and his need to sit down when he is doing his worksheets."
- You take your teenage daughter to an art museum and split up so each family member can visit his or her favorite galleries. An hour later, you find your daughter just where you left her, and there are tears in her eyes. "This single painting carries the essence of what it means to be human," she says. It's then that you realize she has spent her whole time gazing at this one piece of artwork.
- You are packing the last of the boxes on the moving van when you spy your 10-year-old carefully tearing a bit of wallpaper from the living room. Upon closer examination, you see that he has pieces of wallpaper from every room tucked away in a shoebox. "These will help me remember every room in the most special house in the world," he explains to you.
- After your 4-year-old falls in the driveway, scraping her knee, you take her in your arms to comfort her tears. Once soothed, she looks you straight in the eye and says, "Mommy, it's never going to get better than this."

And, what do many people do when they are presented with these intensities? Rather than caress or cherish them, they complain about how "messy" they make life for the individual involved. So, instead of talking with Joey's teacher about ways to channel his intellectual excitement, we come up with behavior charts and fake awards Joey earns if he sits for 20 minutes without leaving his seat. Or, we chastise our daughter for missing out on the new Abyssinian exhibit because she just sat and stared at "a picture, a single, stupid picture" for an hour. We roll our eyes at the wallpaper incident, lecturing about the need not to damage property or take things that no longer belong to us. Finally, we tell our sensitive 4-year-old that she needs to be more careful in the driveway, effectively ignoring the power of her sentiment. In ways both subtle and all-too-obvious, society tries to transform unique perceptions

... by asking gifted children to quiet down their brains, emotions and imaginations, and to see things in more typical ways, we are telling them that the interest is due on their childhood notions and they must "pay up" by relinquishing these views in an effort to fit in with everyday notions of reality. In truth, though, they owe no bill at all. They are just being themselves.

into commonplace, standard-issue behaviors, beliefs, perceptions, and attitudes. When this occurs, we chip away so much of the essence of giftedness that the block that remains is just a remnant of its former self. To tweak the metaphor of this chapter's title just a little more directly, by asking gifted children to "quiet down" their brains, emotions, and imaginations and to see things in more typical ways, we are telling them that the interest is due on their childhood notions and they must "pay up" by relinquishing these views in an effort to fit in with everyday notions of reality. In truth, though, they owe no bill at all. They are just being themselves.

The Wonderful Wizard of OEs

If one person has made the world a little more palatable for those individuals who experience life in a higher key, it is Michael Piechowski. Polish born, Michael immigrated to the United States to pursue two (not just one!) Ph.D.s— the first in molecular biology and the second in counseling psychology. Indeed, who better to know about the inner workings of gifted individuals than someone who has studied them at the molecular level.

Michael came to know a psychiatrist named Kazimierz Dabrowski at his first academic appointment at the University of Alberta. Dabrowski had written extensively, in Polish, on people who experienced life in ways that were more intense and vivid than most. Some of these people Dabrowski studied had been diagnosed with mental illnesses and were perceived as psychoneurotic by physicians who saw their behaviors and perceptions as erratic and odd. Hospitalization and medication were often prescribed to "cure" these individuals.

Dabrowski had another take on this; he did not see mental illness at all, but rather, he saw individuals who were suffering in a different way. As Piechowski recalls:

> Dabrowski felt a great urgency to help and save those who are sensitive, vulnerable, empathetic, and creative, but who are not well adapted to the world where aggressive competition pushes people to get ahead with little consideration for their fellow humans. (Delisle, 2000, p. 218)

Because Dabrowski's books had never been translated adequately into English, these two Polish dynamos met regularly with that as one of their tasks. Eventually, Piechowski gleaned from his mentor the theory of positive integration, a complex structure detailing how some humans systematically achieve areas of self-knowledge and self-actualiza-tion that transcend those of most others. Taking this theory and elaborating upon it with his own brand of realism, Piechowski coined the term *overexcitabilities* (OEs), which is a psychological umbrella encompassing several differ-ent domains of human interaction: psychomotor, sensual, intellectual, imaginational, and emotional. From this point on, the gifted person's proclivities towards overindulgence took on a new spin—a positive one.

The OEs in More Depth

Michael Piechowski jokes that the term OE can stand for two things—overexcitability or original equipment, as the nature of these OEs is inborn in those who have them in abundance. Let's examine the five OEs in greater detail, with an eye toward helping our gifted children better under-stand and appreciate them, in themselves and in others.

Psychomotor Overexcitability

Psychomotor overexcitability is often characterized as a surplus of physical energy that can be seen in a variety of ways: rapid speech with marked excitement ("Ooh! Ooh! Teacher! Pick me! Pick me!"), intense physical activity in organized sports (or simply at recess), and impulsive actions or nervous hab-its, like nail biting or pencil drumming. Piechowski and Cunningham (1985) have found that psychomotor over-excitability alone does not distinguish gifted children from average ones; however, when this physical energy combines with intense intellectual exploration, the result is often an out-of-his-seat whiz kid who grates on his teacher's last nerve. As you might imagine, a misdiagnosis of Attention Deficit/Hyperactivity Disorder (ADHD) is not uncommon for children (and adults) who show these overexcitable signs (Webb et al., 2005). The distinction between a true case of ADHD and the situation of a gifted person who is overexcitable in the psychomotor domain is that the OE individual is able to focus for extended time periods on topics of intellectual interest. When the cognitive juices are flowing, the only ADHD thing about them is that they tend to ignore the mundane distractions of everyday life (. . . like the teacher reciting the night's homework assignment).

Helping your child control these psychomotor impulses can be as difficult as herding cats in an open field, for movement is as natural to them as singing is to a contralto. Giving quieter options is one possibility such as, "Frank, if you must drum with your pencil, hit your legs instead of your desk. The teacher won't hear it." Or, in the case of a child who blurts out in class, "Jen, when an answer comes into your mind, scribble it into your notebook and I promise to get back to you about it later." However, as you might imagine, these gimmicks are temporary fixes, at best. The best solution is not a solution at all, but a situation—find teachers who tolerate movement and encourage it as just another way to learn. So, if your daughter fidgets while sitting at her desk during silent reading, what's the harm in having her stand, or lie down on the pillows in the back of the room, or sit in the rocking chair that most teachers who appreciate kids like this always seem to have in their classrooms? Yes, there is a time and a place for everything, including sitting down and being quiet, but if part of your original equipment involves psychomotor OE, 7 hours of classroom time sitting still is a form of legal torture.

Sensual Overexcitability

Sensual overexcitability should not be confused with raging hormones, that adolescent affliction attributed to any teenager with an emerging libido. Nor is sensual OE a quality observed only in older children, for it can be noted in even the youngest of kids. Do you have a child who cuts the labels off T-shirts because they are too itchy? Do you have a child who smells everything before she eats, wears, or plays with it, announcing, "I like it" (or not), from this mere olfactory experience? Do you have a child who asks the teacher to turn off the fluorescent lights because the incessant buzzing is a constant distraction? Do you have a child (or spouse) who avoids the perfume area in any department store for fear of getting an unwanted, headache-inducing spritz from one of those annoying employees paid to spray unsuspecting victims? These sensually aware individuals have fine-tuned sensory systems that are bombarded by stimuli constantly, each one attractive or repellent in its own unique way.

Consider this piece, written by an 11-year-old as part of his collection of scientific poetry:

Fall Leaves

By Robert J.

I see a leaf
It is yellow with red and orange mixed in
My mind says: "the yellow is caused by the oxidation of leftover sugars
The red and orange are caused by the emergence of recessive pigments."
I see a leaf
It is yellow with red and orange mixed in
My heart says: "the yellow is a bit of leftover sun from summer
The red and orange is the leaf spiraling down the lower spectrum

As it is going to sleep."
I see a leaf.

Beautiful words and images, to be sure. But, what it took for Robert to create them involved more than just interesting, sophisticated wordplay. It also took an enhanced ability to sense the world from multiple perspectives—to see a leaf in all its formations.

Children who are sensually overexcitable might be criticized as being too dramatic, too sensitive, too everything! To help them appreciate the beauty of this gift of insight, let them explore avenues that relish this savvy; let them paint, act, write, sing, and create images of the world that they sense in a higher key than others. Too, give them appropriate outlets for dealing with situations that are overly loud or boisterous. One family I know convinced their daughter's kindergarten teacher that she be allowed to leave the gym during assemblies and simply sit in the adjacent hallway. There, she reads quietly, often with her hands on her ears, until the ruckus has subsided. Now tell me, wouldn't *you* do the same if you could at that rock concert or monster truck rally someone dragged you to against your better judgment? Personal preference, personal need: In the case of sensual OE, that's the name of the game.

Intellectual Overexcitability

Having an *intellectual overexcitability* would seem to be synonymous with giftedness and that is, in fact, very close to true. As I described in an earlier publication,

The intellectually OE person is a minefield of exploding thoughts. It is someone who is curious, mentally alert even when relaxing, driven to absorb and understand any new idea, and someone who likes any type of intellectual challenge, be they word games, three-dimensional puzzles, or the College Championship segments on *Jeopardy!*. The intellectually OE child will be in bed at the appropriate bedtime but will more likely than not be reading under the covers with a flashlight. (Delisle, 2000, pp. 222–223)

Always asking "Why?" even from the youngest of ages, and not being satisfied with pat answers that are incomplete or simply not true, the intellectually OE person is on cognitive overdrive constantly. They are challenging, too. Not afraid to take on untruths that are disguised as "authority," they will correct their teachers, their parents, and their friends. They point out inconsistencies in thinking and will be among the first to recognize when the Emperor is not wearing any clothes. Stupidity makes them angry. Illogic makes them cringe.

The best thing that a parent can do when confronted by an intellectually OE child is to listen. They will share theories and ideas. They will read to you page after page of their latest favorite book so you can gain a flavor for its importance. They will complain about adults who offer wrong information, but refuse to admit it even when presented with a factual rebuttal. And, if they are in a school that neither challenges them nor appreciates their willingness to argue, they will beg you to send them elsewhere or to begin home schooling.

Encourage this ambitious love of learning, but let your son or daughter know that there is a time and a place for everything. So, it is better to go to a teacher after class and correct her syntax privately, rather than to do it in front of 25 other seventh graders. Also, let them know that the bus ride home is probably not the best time to inform your classmates about the distinction between a Russian and a Prussian. Finally, forget about correcting Dad's grammar at the dinner table when he is retelling (again) his favorite story about growing up in Appalachia. Going back to Hollingworth's notion of suffering fools gladly, the situations above would be handy-dandy times to recall her warning about getting martyred by the mob.

Can someone be gifted and not overexcitable intellectually? That depends on your definition of giftedness, of course. To me, an example of this is the high achieving student who earns perfect grades, but whose intellectual curiosity is dormant—the child who says, out loud or through actions, "Just tell me how to earn the A and I'm outta here." Missing out on the richness that accompanies an intellectually OE person, a high achiever like this is no more gifted than any scribbled sketch is a Picasso.

Imaginational Overexcitability

If you live with a child who possesses *imaginational* OE, your life is filled with frolic. Your imaginative child lives in the kingdom of creativity, manufacturing parallel universes and inventing friends who live in them. When asked at school to name the four basic food groups, your child might respond "Burger King, Pizza Hut, McDonald's, and Wendy's," just because it is a more interesting answer than the typical one teachers seek. In your child's mind, the only thing absurd is the ordinary, the only second language worth learning is one you've invented, and the most important question that is ever asked is not "Why?" but "Why not?" Their idol is Jim Carrey.

There is also a painful part of being an imaginationally OE child—lots of people don't "get you." Such a child's humor is often tinged with irony or double entendres, and they may guffaw at situations that those with less active imaginations fail to see as funny. A case in point: Six-year-old Cassie was watching a movie on schoolyard safety being shown by her physical education teacher. As the teacher went to turn off the VCR, he tripped over the power cord, falling face first into a first grader's desk. While the rest of the children showed concern about the teacher's safety, Cassie was trying unsuccessfully to stifle a very big laugh. While being admonished by the classroom teacher for laughing at someone's misfortune, Cassie tried to explain (also unsuccessfully) that she found it hilarious that the PE teacher got hurt while showing a movie about safety! Her humor fell far short of impressing the teacher, and a punishment was imposed. I guess when you are 6, you are not supposed to see the humor in situations that would make most adults laugh out loud.

More than anything else, what a child with a strong imaginational OE requires is someone who will encourage this creative spark and not let it die among cries to "get real," "return to Earth," or "think logically, for a change." Put down by a society that only respects creativity when it does not press too strongly on accepted norms, the imaginationally OE child is in danger of repressing this fragile gift to satisfy the swarms of others who wear creative blinders. Remind your child that it is fresh ideas and innovative spirits that will take our world into places not yet reached by conventional thinking. Given a choice of having their imagination channeled or cherished, always go with the latter.

Emotional Overexcitability

The final OE is called *emotional overexcitability*. Alec was 11 years old when the terror of September 11, 2001, took place. As his teacher, I wanted to gain some insights into his and his classmates' innermost feelings about this tragedy, as healing begins with the acknowledgment that you hurt.

I distributed a newspaper photograph of a rescue worker at the World Trade Center. In it, the man was leaning on a railing and, even though you could not see his face, you could feel his anguish. My prompt for the children was to continue this sentence, "In New York City, a rescue worker . . . " Here's what Alec wrote:

> . . . is praying to God. He's not sure if there is a God anymore, but faith won't stop working his miracle on him. He is a hero. He isn't hungry for glory, fame or money, he wants his life back.

> In New York City, a rescue worker is tired. He gets his energy by the heroes around him, and they get their energy from him.

> In New York City, a hero is crying. Heroes do cry.

Ladies and gentlemen, welcome to Alec's world of emotional overexcitability. While most of his classmates wrote a literal interpretation of the photo—"the man is tired and hungry and he hasn't seen his family in a few days"—Alec took these obvious reactions as givens, and he brought his response to a different place, inside the man's soul.

A clinical interpretation of what an emotionally OE child is like would read like this: Intense positive and negative feelings; an awareness of the emotions of others; strong physical reactions to situations that are wrong and need to be corrected; feelings of guilt and shame over being unable to control events that impact others negatively; a capacity for developing strong attachments and deep relationships; and a concern with life, death, God, and spirituality.

The list could go on, but it probably doesn't need to, for if you are the parent of one of these emotionally enriched children, you have already seen him or her in the statements above.

The cornerstone of all of the other OEs, emotional OE is often detected the earliest in gifted children (Lind, 2001), and the most profound in intensity when it appears. It may be interwoven with the other OEs, so that a child who cries in pleasure at the sound of a symphony orchestra is exhibiting rich human emotion brought on by a sensual experience. Seldom selfish and often altruistic, children with emotional OE are the ones who will befriend stray cats or kids who look funny "because someone needs to like them." They want to know why world peace is considered a pipe dream, instead of a goal toward which we should strive. They don't understand why politics gets in the way of buying hungry people food or old people their prescription drugs. As they mature in age, children with emotional OE can become either zealots for righteous causes or embittered to inaction by the barriers put up to what they see as common sense solutions to issues they cherish. More than anything else, gifted children with emotional OE are people you are proud to know, as they possess a rare and uncanny ability to transcend their own lives and act in accordance with principles that are bigger than they. As spouses, parents, community leaders, and quiet advocates for those without a voice, their actions improve a world very much in need of their insights and intensities.

I serve as Alec's teacher still, even though he is no longer in my classroom—not even my school. And, Alec serves as my teacher, too. This symbiotic relationship built on a genuine regard for self and an unwavering respect for human dignity will be with us always. The bond is permanent and secure. When you get to know a child with a similar emotional OE, you will know the true meaning of joy.

The Journey Begins . . .

Each of the OEs described here helps to understand more fully the inner world of the gifted child. Some would call these abilities *emotional intelligence*, a term coined by Daniel Goleman (1995) in his best selling book of the same name, but it was Michael Piechowski who took this idea a step further by postulating that the OEs are not a supplement to the gifted child's personality, but they are the true essence of it. Just as one hand enfolds the other to create a cocoon of warmth, the OEs, when combined with heightened intelligence, create an individual who is capable of both great insights and profound compassion; it becomes hard to distinguish whether the genesis of one's enriched abilities is in the head or the heart. Listen to one father describe his son's reaction to an everyday event:

> When David was 8, he was looking at a picture of his Cub Scout den from a skit they did. David noticed that there was not a space represented in the name "Tiger Cubs." Each boy had one of these letters, and then stepped forward to say something like "T is for Teamwork," etc.
>
> The conversation went something like this:
>
> "Dad, we should have had a space, because "Tiger Cubs" is two words."
>
> "You're right, David, but who would want to be a space?"
>
> Five minutes later, David returned and said, "Dad, they could say:
>
> > 'I am a space
> > I separate Death and Life

Joy and Sadness
Good and Bad
Warmth and Coldness.'

David did this within one week of his eighth birthday. (Personal e-mail correspondence, March 18, 2003)

Was David *taught* how to see this clearly? Did he learn from watching and listening to older children and adults as they explored complex, abstract ideas? If these questions have definitive answers, I have yet to find them. However, such discovery is not the point. Instead, we must realize and accept a simple truth: The giftedness expressed by our children is a quality no more universal than being tall or blue-eyed, and it is no more present in everyone than is having an ear for music, an eye for art, or a heart for empathy. Most importantly, you cannot *train* someone to be gifted, you can only cherish and protect the insights and visions they possess naturally. In essence, gifted children *simply are*.

In closing, I have to wonder, as you read this chapter, did you envision the discussion of giftedness going in the direction that it did? Most books about giftedness review in overblown detail the intricacies of IQ and achievement tests and the benefits and flaws of each in the identification of high intelligence. Instead, I took you on a different kind of ride and led you, I hope, to a different kind of place. The destination I sought was self-discovery that involved a vision of giftedness more complex and less well-defined than most. Pinpointing its definition is hard, but knowing when you see it is easy. As Michael Piechowski (1991) wrote,

When gifted people, and those who live and work with them, are introduced to these OE concepts, there is often an instant recognition and a sense of relief. It helps to find out that there is a theoretical model that makes sense out of a manner of feeling and acting that is so often at odds with normal behavior and expectations of happy—or grim, as the case may be—adjustment. It helps for once to feel legitimate in one's "abnormal" reactions and what one cannot help experiencing and wanting to express. (p. 287)

The formation of the OEs is lifelong in nature. For better or for worse, they are never outgrown, but more on that in a later chapter on adult giftedness.

Gifted Children Speak Out

"I've found that one part of my personal myth is the belief in myself, my abilities, and my thought processes. I am a spiritual being, capable of great wisdom, deep thought, and personal happiness. I look into myself for answers, and often find pieces of myself that I never realized existed. I put them into the puzzle of my life, and hope that one day the masterpiece will be complete."

—Boy, age 17

"I do worry about problems—not so much for the world, but more for things at school. I worry because kids get teased no matter what they look, dress, or act like."

—Girl, age 13

"I think I see the world differently. I don't care about what you saw on TV or who you are going out with. I'm not interested in team sports or big parties. I'd rather read a book. I like to think. I care about my grades. I like to be left alone."

—Girl, age 14

Chapter 4

Take Charge of Your Child's Education

My K–8 education was in a small Catholic school with huge class sizes. A neighboring parochial school had burned to the ground when I was in fourth grade, so all of its students descended upon our building, swelling our body count even more. Looking back, I cannot fathom how one young nun was able to teach and control the more than 50 of us who sat in her combined fourth and fifth grade room for the better part of 2 years.

But, I do remember this: Sister Patricia broke the rigid stereotype of grade level placement by allowing those students who could handle the lessons to migrate from one side of our classroom to the other. So, in handwriting, I was still in fourth grade (and should still be!), but in spelling and reading and math, I was in fifth. It finally got to the point where my seat was changed, and I was placed in the classroom's middle row, the one that mingled together kids from both grades. "Just listen when I teach the fifth graders," Sister Patricia whispered to me, "I think you'll do just fine."

Thus was my first exposure to grade and content acceleration, and to a teacher who understood the benefits of both.

Of all the complaints you are likely to hear from your gifted children, boredom in school is probably going to top the list. Occasionally, the boredom will be feigned, as the students are just not appreciating content that is at their level, but not on their radar screens in terms of interest. Too, there will be times when a gifted child says, "I'm bored," as justification for not doing homework that, frankly, they do not know how to do. (When you're a smart kid, it's tough to admit any academic gaps to others). And, of course, there are those gifted kids who say they are bored because it is just the cool thing to say in front of their classmates. Hey, who wants to hang out with a gifted geek who begs for additional learning matter the way Oliver pleaded for more food ("Please, Sir, more worksheets . . . ")?

> In an era where federal legislation and state-level mandates prescribe that all children learn to read, compute, and compose at preset, minimal levels, the needs of gifted children are being bypassed.

Often, though, the boredom is justified; gifted kids wait around for others to finish work that they completed in half the allotted time; or they are taking their umpteenth quiz on state capitals in fourth grade, even though they could recite and locate each one by the end of kindergarten; or they are being asked to regurgitate who-was-who in the Civil War, rather than discussing if that war eradicated racism or simply made it take on more subtle forms after Reconstruction.

One thing is certain: In an era where federal legislation and state-level mandates prescribe that all children learn to read, compute, and compose at preset, minimal levels, the needs of gifted children are being bypassed. As we try to determine ways to leave no child behind who struggles to learn, we are (choose your term):

> neglecting . . .
> ignoring . . .
> caring less about . . .
> slapping in the face . . .

those children for whom learning comes rapidly and readily. In too many instances, the educational needs of gifted children are forgotten, as our collective emphasis in schools is not to measure how tall the tree, but how tall the stump.

This chapter could be one slam after another at politicians and other noneducators who think they know what is best for children they have never taught, but I'll leave that battle for elsewhere. Here, I intend to give several reasons why gifted child education is in the current quagmire that it is, and then provide concrete ways to advocate for your gifted child's needs in whatever school situation he finds himself, whether an elite and expensive private school, the neighborhood high school, or Sister Patricia's classroom of 50 children.

The "Error" of Inclusion

Dalton Conley, in his stunning book *Honky* (2000), describes what it was like to grow up as the only White boy in the projects on the Lower East Side of Manhattan in the late 1970s. By lying about his address to a New York City bureaucracy too large to know any better, Conley's parents managed to get him transferred to a Greenwich Village elementary school inhabited by professors' kids from New York University. His education there was different from his schooling in the slums, but was it better?

I spent so much time on my geography and math fixations that I did almost no schoolwork. The only problems that interested me were ones that weren't already solved. I had not yet learned that eight times nine was seventy-two, but I didn't care, because everybody already knew that. The time I was supposed to be memorizing multiplication tables I spent trying to break the four-color map rule. I had decided there was no point in doing anything that was not original, that wasn't big, really big. My grades were mediocre, and my teacher consistently claimed on my report card that I was not "performing up to my potential." (p. 72–73)

So, who is the underachiever, Dalton, or the curriculum he was expected to "learn"?

I began my teaching career just a few years shy of Dalton Conley's experiences in urban schools. Back then, if his intelligence had been noted as high (which it undoubtedly is), Dalton would likely have been channeled to a "special class," a learning environment where children of similar intellects gathered to explore, among other things, the four-color map rule. Similar to special educational settings for children with disabilities, kids who either struggled to learn or excelled at it were segmented off from the general population, for all or part of each day. The end result was children being served about as appropriately as can be expected in heterogeneous public schools. Teachers were now serving students in milieus where the intellectual range was rather narrow: slow, average, and smart in different classes.

Of course, this common sense approach could not last forever. Cries of elitism and discrimination were charged by critics—several of them valid, most of them not. In some cases, middle class White kids inhabited the "smart class," while the class for children with learning difficulties was populated disproportionately by poor kids or kids of other ethnicities. Instead of examining how this imbalance could be corrected by looking at children's strengths or deficiencies in nontraditional ways, the entire model of separating children by ability and need was dissed: *dismissed, discounted, distrusted.* The reaction of the children affected? *Disgust.*

In place of these classrooms where a child's ability level was considered before placement was made, all kids were now thrown together into a big, messy pool called *inclusion.* More of an experiment in social change than in educational equity, inclusion placed fourth graders who could read at the 10th-grade level with youngsters who were still learning to write complete sentences. In the middle, of course, were fourth graders functioning at levels expected for their age, and in front of them all was a teacher, a trained professional educator. Trouble is, in a situation like this, what you need is a trained professional juggler. Seeing a range so wide and needs so diverse in the student body, many teachers did what they thought was best—they taught to the middle. Sure, some kids were bored and others were confused, but what alternative was there for a teacher at wit's end?

Enter the grand solutions, the panaceas to end all panaceas, *differentiation* and *cooperative learning*! Taking the best gifted child education had to offer—advanced content, open-ended assignments, activities involving higher level and critical thinking skills—teachers were told that differentiation was the way to address the needs of *all* students, regardless of current level of academic functioning. So, if gifted students needed a challenge, teachers were told to provide enrichment materials that differed from the regular curriculum. And, if some of the struggling students found grade level work too rigorous, teachers could locate some high-interest, low vocabulary books that taught the same content and develop tests and quizzes that measured what these kids picked up through silent reading. Better still, have the less capable students work with the "smart kids" in cooperative learning groups. Not only will everyone learn, everyone will learn the value of another's contributions to a group process, and everyone will learn that important social skill of accepting individual differences!

Of course, differentiation and cooperative learning were, and continue to be, the equivalents of an educational trainwreck for gifted students. How could they not? Similar to the mayhem of an emergency room on a busy summer night, where triage is overwhelmed by cases of cuts and bruises, heart attacks, sun stroke, and broken limbs, there is no one person—physician or teacher—who can handle well all the conflicting, compounding needs being presented. For effective treatment, experts need to be on call and available, and separating the most severe cases from the mild problems will need to occur. Makes sense in hospitals, makes sense in schools.

> The error of inclusion and its ragtag "solutions" of differentiation and cooperative learning have done enormous harm . . . If schools were like hospitals, malpractice suits would be rampant.

This error of inclusion and its ragtag "solutions" of differentiation and cooperative learning have done enormous harm to the appropriate education of gifted children—*your* gifted children. If schools were like hospitals, malpractice suits would be rampant.

Where to Turn?

The irony of this situation is that we know both the cause of the problem and some workable alternatives, yet not much is being done to correct what we know is wrong. However, in 2004, a big step forward was taken when a national report on this travesty was released. *A Nation Deceived: How Schools Hold Back America's Brightest Students* (Colangelo, Assouline, & Gross, 2004) sent out a loud cry that may yet be heard. In titling their first chapter "America Ignores Excellence," the authors contend—and they have the data to back them up—that while Rome burns, educationally speaking, school leaders are fiddling away:

> America's school system keeps bright students in line by forcing them to learn in a lock-step manner with their classmates. Teachers and principals disregard students' desires to learn more—much more—than they are being taught.
>
> Instead of praise and encouragement, these students hear one word—no. When they ask for a challenge, they are held back. When they want to fly, they are told to stay in their seats.
>
> Stay in your grade. Know your place.
>
> It's a national scandal. And the price may be the slow and steady erosion of American excellence. (p. 1)

OK—maybe a little too much saber-rattling and hyperbole in those words, but the intention is legitimate: Let gifted students get on with their education by doing what Sister Patricia did with me so long ago—skip content I already knew and allow, indeed, encourage, me to move at my own pace through new material. Who would accompany me on this quest? Other kids who had similar or higher abilities, and teachers who saw the benefit of aligning my abilities with the content being delivered to me in school.

As Yogi Berra might say, "It's déjà vu all over again!"

Like any national report, its effects are only worthwhile if the research-based suggestions are brought to the attention of the decision makers—in this case, school boards and district administrators. Show them page 2 of this report (which is available for free; see http://nationdeceived.org), which highlights the "20 most important points" about acceleration, including that it is cost-free and that it benefits gifted children, both academically and socially. Introduce them to the Iowa Acceleration Scale (Assouline, Colangelo, Lupkowski-Shoplik, & Forstadt, 2003), an instrument that provides a systematic and thorough method for educators and parents who are considering grade-skipping students in grades K–8. Read through Chapter 10 on public policy and attitudes about acceleration so you will be prepared when a naysayer mentions how "undemocratic" or "emotionally damaging" acceleration is for children. Above all else, if you have a gifted child whose educational needs are not being served in a school where the academic brakes are being applied every time he wants to speed up, remember this oft-forgotten reality: Moving along at a pace that accommodates one's learning abilities does not involve accelerating as much as it does catching up. Water seeks its own level and, when it finds it, it flows freely and smoothly. So does intellect.

A Word on Teacher Bashing

One of the biggest mistakes parents of gifted children make in trying to get their children an appropriate education is to blame the teacher when things do not go right. Sure, there are educators who think the worst thing that ever happened to schools was unbolting desks from the floor, but the majority of teachers share a common perspective—they want to do what is best for their students.

Granted, their idea of *best* and yours may differ—a little or a lot. Please remember this: Because there is virtually *no* information provided about gifted children during an undergraduate teacher training program, and because professional development for practicing teachers rarely has the needs of gifted students in mind, many educators are simply doing one of two things—what a gifted coordinator tells them to do, or "punting" by relying on past experiences with other gifted students they have taught. Remember, too, that in today's politically charged schools, maximum achievement is less of a focus than minimum competency, so the pressure to reach a school's highest academic all-stars is limited to school personnel who realize the importance of reaching both ends of the intellectual spectrum.

I've yet to meet a teacher who plans lessons where one of the objectives is to bore the students. In the next section, I will review ways to approach school personnel if you would like to see some changes in your child's education, but for now, bear one thing in mind—teachers are there to reach children, not alienate them from the learning process.

The Underground Guide to Getting Your Way

Having just written what I did, I am now going to write about an incident where I did not take my own best advice. Call it editorial license.

My wife and I were once (and only once, I believe) called "pushy parents" because of an unnecessary confrontation that occurred between our gifted son and one of his teachers. A compliant student and a strong one, Matt experienced a middle school math teacher who decided that despite our son's straight-A average, he wasn't taking notes the way she had prescribed them to be written. In an attempt to appease this teacher, Matt would come home and recopy his notes into the teacher's format. Matt knew he would never use these notes, but this 1 hour or longer nightly task would earn him 20% of his grade. Matt felt pressured to comply.

When we discovered this unnecessary exercise, which was preventing Matt from focusing on both worthwhile homework and enjoying some purposeful downtime after school, we asked him to approach his teacher about not having to complete this assignment. He had done so already, he informed us, and even when presented with the logic of Matt's being a top student in this honors-level class, his teacher emphasized how her structure of note taking was superior to his. "You need to take notes the way I tell you," she said. Matt's frustration continued, as did ours.

To make what could be a long story short, my wife and I approached this teacher—first separately, then together—about the reasonableness of her request. She treated us with the same condescending attitude that she had shown our son—"I *am* the teacher, you know"—and even when we brought our request to the principal, his milquetoast response was that "when it comes to academics, I support my staff." So, despite our combined five degrees in education and more than 30 years of experience as teachers, we were written off as malcontents; pushy parents who just couldn't see beyond their own child's whining. Imagine the reception we might have received had we "only" been blue-collar workers!

Eventually, we told Matt to choose whether or not to complete this silly assignment and that we would support him if he chose not to; whatever grade he earned in this class would be fine with us. How ironic: We gave our son permission to circumvent an educational system that we had supported for years, all because tenure prevailed over logic. The story ended well, as Matt survived seventh-grade math and experienced an eighth-grade teacher whose philosophy was, "Hey, if he can show me how he got his answer differently from mine, I'll learn something!" Still, that school system lost two advocates when it turned a deaf ear to our reasoned request, as they refused to show us or our son the most essential element in successful school-home relationships—respect.

And that, dear reader, is often the basis for any strained relations between a parent of a gifted child and the school—feeling, as a parent, that your knowledge of your child's needs and abilities is ignored in deference to a belief that *all* children need to do things in certain ways and at prescribed times. That's not just an illusion, it's disrespect.

So, how *do* you get your voice heard in such ways that your child benefits from your intervention? Here are some suggested strategies that we and other parents have used to good effect.

Never Request a Teacher, Always Request a Style

Principals hate when parents come to them and request a specific teacher for the following year. More a situation in elementary schools than in higher grades, this practice pits well-connected parents against each other, as each vies to get that one teacher who works best with gifted kids like yours. The problems in requesting a specific teacher are many. First, unless you know this teacher well, the fit might not be a good one for your child—hey, the seventh-grade math czarina I wrote about above had several parent advocates who would have recommended her for gifted children. Second, there are only so many "slots" in your preferred teacher's class, and most principals are reluctant to put all of the "smart kids" in one place. Racial and gender balance, among other factors, must be considered in class placement decisions. Third, new teachers are hired all the time, and veteran teachers shift grade levels regularly. Requesting one particular teacher months in advance may limit the range of good options that would be open to your child. So, instead of asking for a particular teacher . . .

. . . request a particular style. For example, saying to the principal, "My daughter is a quick and independent learner and very organized. I've found she works best in situations where she is given clear direction, but then allowed to pursue her work at her own pace. Is there a teacher on your staff who works best with a child like my little girl?" Or, perhaps your case is more like this: "I know my son; he is bright, but he needs structure. He needs to know his limits and what is due when. He is working at about two grade levels above his class placement, so do you have a teacher who can provide a good balance of challenge and organization?"

> The surest way to raise the hairs on your child's teachers' necks is to use the word *bored* . . . I can't fix bored any more than I could expect my auto mechanic to repair my car by simply stating, "It's broken."

Mentioning how your child learns best will have the principal thinking through his or her staff for a good fit. Still, it provides the wiggle room and the independence to make an administrative decision that is, truth be told, one that is the principal's to make. Your nonrequest is a respectful way to get a teacher who will work well with both your child's skills and personality.

Strike the Words *Bored* and *Not Challenged* From Your Vocabulary

The surest way to raise the hairs on your child's teachers' necks is to use the word *bored* in their presence. The biggest reason teachers (myself included) detest this word is its implication: I am doing something intentionally to turn your child off to learning. I can't fix bored any more than I could expect my auto mechanic to repair my car by simply stating, "It's broken." The terms bored and broken are too vague—more specifics are needed if the kid or the car is to run properly again.

If your child announces (often with a dramatic flair worthy of an Emmy) that boredom is an issue, ask for details: Is the work too easy? Too hard (yes, this can also cause boredom)? Irrelevant to life outside of school? Not an area of personal interest? Once you have ascertained some specifics, ask the next question, "If you could make this class better, what would *you* do?" If your child is unable or unwilling to pinpoint the direct causes of the boredom or its solution, present to him or her this reality, "I can only help you if you give me some examples—being bored is just too vague."

Having this dialogue with your child helps in a couple of ways. First, it gives her some time to think about and articulate why school is dull and how it could be better. Also, it helps her to become, with some effort, part of the solution. Boredom is a very enervating condition, sapping the vitality out of any potential learning than might go on if interest were higher. By giving your child the responsibility of dissecting the boring situation into its component parts, you are heading in a positive direction, as you (or your child) can now approach the teacher with a suggestion or two for change.

Of course, this is predicated on your child's teacher(s) being willing to listen to reason. I find it rare, though, for a teacher to ignore a child's request for doing different, often more difficult, work if a plan is made for what is to be done, how it will be done, and by when. Too, the alternative assignments or work may have to relate to the curriculum being studied, but some teachers, if they know your child understands the basic material, will give them a freer rein to do something a bit more exotic or esoteric.

Just a word about the term *not challenged*: This is merely a more polite way of saying bored, so don't use it, either. The same solutions apply, though; figure out the sources of the lack of challenge and arrive at ways to address it with other, valuable activities. Not only does this place the student in the driver's seat for his or her own learning, in gives the teacher a roadmap to help the student reach an interesting destination.

Know the Jargon

Every field has it, and gifted child education is no exception: jargon. To become legitimate jargon, the terms need multiple syllables and, even better, they should be difficult to pronounce. Here are just a few you might want to learn, as they are common terms in this uncommon field. Table 1 provides definitions for several of these, plus definitions for other jargon you might hear in the field of gifted education.

- acceleration and enrichment (and the differences between the two);
- differentiation and curriculum compacting (hint: the latter does not deal with trash);
- Bloom's Taxonomy (not as confusing as it sounds);
- least restrictive environment versus most appropriate environment (the first is a term from special education, the latter refers to where gifted children are best served);
- cluster grouping, self-contained classes, and pull-out programs (three of the many ways kids are grouped to receive gifted services);
- Parallel Curriculum Model, Enrichment Triad Model, Destination Imagination, Schoolwide Enrichment Model, and Autonomous Learner Model (organized plans to serve gifted students—some better than others—and none of which should be used exclusively); and
- multiple criteria, screening, and identification (know

the difference), and quantitative and qualitative assessment (these all have to do with placement decisions for gifted children).

A good source for understanding these and other terms is *Re-forming Gifted Education*, a book by Karen Rogers (2002). Karen even goes so far as to include charts with underground information like, "If a teacher/administrator says this, this is what you say back." This book, and your knowledge of the terms that will be thrown about with any professional who understands gifted education, will make you a more informed parent. Speaking the language, educationally speaking, helps to even out what is sometimes an uneven playing field of jargon.

Unite for a Common Good and a Common Goal

Having lived in the northern U.S. my entire life, I understand a simple, winter reality: A snowflake falling here or there doesn't alter my travel plans at all, but when a lot of these snowflakes get together, they can create havoc with my schedule.

Now, this may seem an odd analogy in advocating for your gifted child; first, I do not (generally) see parents as flakes, and second, the goal of advocating for your child's appropriate education is not (again, generally) to create chaos in the schools. The point of the snowflake analogy is simply this: There is strength in numbers. Parents of children with disabilities learned this long ago. Today, legislation is in place and budgets have swelled to make certain the special needs of kids with disabilities are addressed. Much of the reason behind this surge in special education is that parents rose up and said, collectively, "our children are not served well in the public schools, their civil rights are being violated, and *you will* do something about it."

Table 1
Common Terms Used in Gifted Education,
and What They Mean to You

Ability grouping: Grouping students of like ability to work together on a short- or long-term basis.

Acceleration: Allowing students to move to a higher level of schoolwork than their age would ordinarily dictate. This can be in the form of early entry to school, placement in a self-contained gifted classroom, earning credit by passing an examination, skipping grades, completing two grades in a single year, or dual-enrollment in both high school and college. Students can also be accelerated in specific subject areas for single classes (i.e., taking seventh-grade-level math when the student is in the sixth grade).

Assessment: The process of evaluating student learning with standardized testing and a clearly defined portfolio of individual work samples. Gifted education teachers often attempt to evaluate student work or performance in order to tailor their teaching to student needs and interests.

Bloom's Taxonomy: Created by Benjamin Bloom in 1956, it's the classification of thinking into six levels of increasing complexity: knowledge, comprehension, application, analysis, synthesis, and evaluation.

Cluster grouping: Small instructional groups consisting of students of the same grade level who have been identified as gifted, but have been placed in a classroom of otherwise heterogeneously grouped students.

Curriculum compacting: Compacting is an adaptation to the curriculum that shortens or eliminates work that students have already mastered quicker than their classmates. It allows students the additional time and opportunity they need for enrichment or acceleration options. This process is sometimes called telescoping.

Table 1 continued

Differentiation: Adapting the pace, level, or kind of instructional curriculum to meet each student's individual learning needs, styles, or interests.

Enrichment: Generic term for a range of challenging student learning opportunities outside of the regular curriculum. Enrichment can also take place outside of the school system.

Flexible grouping: Grouping students based on their interests and abilities on an assignment-by-assignment basis.

Heterogeneous grouping: Also referred to as mixed-ability grouping, this is when students with differing abilities, achievements, interests, perspectives, and backgrounds are grouped together.

Homogeneous grouping: Also referred to as like-ability grouping, this is when students of similar ability are grouped together, regardless of their age.

Identification: Various methods used to determine which students are best suited for gifted services and programs.

IQ (intelligence quotient): Measure of a child's cognitive ability that compares a child's mental age and actual age.

Learning style: A student's preferred mode of learning, such as auditory, tactile, visual, or kinesthetic.

Least restrictive environment (LRE): The educational setting where a child with disabilities can receive a free, appropriate public education designed to meet his or her needs. LRE also requires that these students be educated with peers without disabilities in the regular classroom environment.

Table 1 continued

Multiple intelligences: Originally identified by psychologist Howard Gardner in his theory of multiple intelligences, this encompasses different ways of learning and processing information. The eight intelligences (as identified by Gardner) are linguistic, musical, logical-mathematical, visual-spatial, bodily-kinesthetic, interpersonal, intrapersonal, and naturalistic. Each individual has relative strengths and weaknesses within these domains.

Multipotentiality: Concept that gifted children have the ability to succeed in several areas of work or study, making career selection difficult.

Pull-out programs: This is a part-time program where gifted children leave their regular classrooms to attend specialized classes with a resource teacher. Also referred to as resource-room and send-out programs.

Self-contained program: When students are grouped on a full-time basis with intellectual peers, often for consecutive years. Its aim is to promote high achievement and reduce the social and emotional issues that gifted children may face.

Standardized testing: Testing of students under identical conditions that allows for results to be statistically compared to a standard.

Tracking: Permanently grouping students by ability, such as in the "low," "middle," or "high" math group.

Twice-exceptional: Quality of being both gifted and having a physical, emotional, or learning disability.

Underachievement: School performance that falls short of a student's ability.

Note. Compiled from Delisle & Lewis, 2003, and LRE Coalition, 2005.

Funny thing . . . parents of gifted children could say the same things, but they often don't.

Why not? There are a couple of reasons. First (and I realize this sounds very tacky), gifted kids do not get the "sympathy vote" that other children with special needs do. No one begrudges children who are mentally handicapped the right to be taught in ways that will help them learn as much as they can, but in comparison, when you have a "smart kid," you are likely to hear from others, "Oh! What a joy it must be to have a gifted child. You must be so thankful!" That sympathetic rug has just been swept from under you, and your impassioned cry in the wilderness for equal treatment for your child is met with raised eyebrows and an unstated "just be happy with what you got." This lack of understanding about the specific needs of gifted children has probably caused more parents to keep their mouths closed than any other reason.

Too, when education dollars are limited, as they always are, some parents of gifted children actually feel guilty that they seek funds for kids whose needs, by comparison, may not seem as pressing as some other groups of children. The incorrect assumption is that "these kids are smart; they'll make it on their own." Some will, others won't, and as Jim and Shelagh Gallagher (1994) wrote:

> Failure to help gifted children reach their potential is a societal tragedy, the extent of which is difficult to measure but which is surely great. How can we measure the loss of the sonata unwritten, the curative drug undiscovered, or the absence of political insight? These gifted students are a substantial part of the difference between what we are and what we could be as a society. (p. 4)

To make a difference that extends beyond the tenure of your child's school career, you and other parents of gifted children must get together and present your views to a sometimes reluctant audience—a school board strapped with competing demands for priorities, a principal who tells you with a glint in her eye and a cocky smile, "all children are gifted in our school," or a PTO president who doesn't believe a talk about gifted children is an appropriate topic for a meeting, as the audience appeal is too limited. There are two ways to start coalescing parents of gifted children into a (somewhat) cohesive whole; either talk to the gifted coordinator in your school district and ask to have a meeting scheduled where parents of identified gifted kids can have a forum for discussion of common issues, or review one of the many books or Web sites that exist about how parents can unite for the common good of their children and follow the advice of those who came before you (see Appendix A).

Now the bad news: I predict that 90% or more of the people reading this book will not take my advice about advocacy, citing everything from too busy a schedule to being afraid to ruffle the feathers of the school bureaucracy. Too bad, as you will never know the impact you might have made had you taken the time to do what every other special interest group who left a dent in our society has done: speak up to right a wrong. The Gallagher and Gallagher (1994) quote cited above should be ample evidence that the job of getting gifted children the type of education they need is too important to leave to chance or to individual cries for helping a specific child. Together, like snowflakes falling over time, parents of gifted children can demand attention. Indeed, they must.

Conclusion

Taking charge of your child's education is likely to be a time consuming process. Many gifted kids will float through school with nary a complaint—nor will they be learning much of anything. You need to ask yourself, "Is this good enough?" Many gifted teenagers will want you to back off and let them slide through school with easily obtained A's from teachers who don't know the extent of your child's abilities. You need to ask yourself, "Is this good enough?" More than a few gifted children will sleep through class, get demoted to nonhonors classes due to low grades, and be called lazy by educators who have never taken the time to kindle the sparks you know are there. You need to ask yourself, "Is this good enough?"

> Remember this: Parenting is not a passive process.

Each kid gets one childhood. There are no "do-overs" and no second chances to be 9 years old for just one more year. As you make your decision to intervene (or not) when you see your gifted child's needs are being ignored, or as you decide whether (or not) to applaud the efforts of any educator who takes an interest in seeing that your child's mind be challenged fully, remember this: Parenting is not a passive process. Active involvement is the best way to ensure that the kid who smiles at you upon crossing the stage at high school graduation has a full mind and a grateful heart, thanks to both teachers and parents who took the time, who took charge.

Gifted Children Speak Out

"School is too easy for me and boring. I am a straight-A student and school just comes naturally to me. Most of the things kids my age are learning now I have already learned and 'learning' them again just makes my day go longer. Even some of the things they're teaching in the advanced classes don't really challenge me. When school gets this boring, the only thing I enjoy is seeing my friends. I really haven't learned anything lately."

—Boy, age 13

"At 18 months, I accompanied my mother to the dentist. He asked me if I liked TV, and I told him I watched *Sesame Street*. He asked what that show was, and I told him it was 'a production of the children's television workshop,' just like they say at the end of the show. Needless to say, he was quite taken aback!"

—Girl, age 15

"Gifted kids should be treated like gifted kids. Not to put other people down, but we need to be around other kids who think like we do."

—Girl, age 12

Chapter 5

Appreciate That Less Than Perfect Is More Than Acceptable

Dear Mom,

I've asked the receptionist to give you this as soon as you get back from your meeting, so you'll know where I am. Mike's mom is taking me home with her. She was the only person available to take me to the emergency room. My arm isn't moving very well because of the bandages, so I hope you can read this okay.

The firemen said the wiring was very old. You'll be glad to know I saved the family album. Fluffy should be okay, but it doesn't look so good for Tigger.

Also, my algebra teacher wants you to give her a call.

Love,
Bobby

P.S. Just kidding! I'm fine, the house is fine, and Fluffy and Tigger are fine. I am getting a D- in algebra, though. What a relief, huh?

Always Read the P.S.

You can read Bobby's letter from a number of vantage points. If you're a stickler who hates surprises, you'll be punishing Bobby for his insolence in making you fret. If you're a fun-lover who thinks practical jokes are the highest form of art, you'll fall over yourself laughing at the wittiness of Bobby's deception. And, if you're a realist, you understand that Bobby is right on target—compared with all the awful things that could happen in life, a D- in seventh-grade algebra is not so bad after all.

Expectations. We all have them for our kids. Whether in the realm of grades, behavior, or the development of a social conscience, we have certain limits for our children. What gets parents of gifted kids in trouble regarding expectations is when their level of acceptability is only understood vaguely by the child, causing a disconnect not even obvious until it's too late. So, when the report card comes home replete with B's and C's, the curfew is broken, or the principal calls with word that your child is correcting his teachers every day in class, you decide it's time for one of those "little talks" that never work out quite the way you intended. As you sit down to chat, the scene already looks confrontational, and before the first tear is shed, threat made, or apology offered, you realize the lines of communication are as weak as a 16 in Blackjack. The conversation goes something like this:

> You: "Son, I know you are capable of work that is better than this."

> Not you: "Dad, you just expect me to be perfect all the time."

> You: "That's not true."

Not You: "Yeah? How about that time I brought home a B on that science project . . . "

You: "You mean the one you threw together at the last minute? I wasn't mad about the grade, I was disappointed with your effort."

Not You: "Yeah . . . like all I ever do all day is just lie around playing video games. I'm in all the honors classes, you know. Sometimes, I just need time to relax."

You: "And you thought that relaxing until the night before your science project was due was a fine way to relieve the pressure?"

Not You (big sigh): "OK, I screwed up. Your little gifted genius can't always cut it. Big surprise—I'm human!"

What follows next is either a stomping out of the room (by either of you), a final parental statement that proves defeat ("You're grounded until I see improvement" is common), or a boatload of tears based in frustration. Saddest of all, the situation was not resolved and "You" and "Not You" still are chasms apart in understanding each other's perspectives on what success looks like. Let's examine some of the underlying reasons that gifted children and their parents often differ on how high is high enough when it comes to achievement in school. Only then can a truce be declared where there are no losers, only winners.

Issue #1A: The Aura of the Gifted Label (Parent Perspective)

Even if you knew your son or daughter was gifted from day one, when such impressions are confirmed by test scores there comes a feeling of pride and relief—your suspicions were confirmed by school personnel who know a gifted kid when they test one. Often, what follows is a honeymoon period where the gifted label is worn proudly (but humbly, of course), and life goes on much as it did before. Like every honeymoon, though, it ends abruptly and reality sets in: There are tests to take, competitions to enter, and academic challenges to master. It's only natural, as a parent, to assume your gifted child will excel at each and every endeavor attempted—hey, that's what being gifted is all about, isn't it? You look around at the other gifted kids, and they seem to have no trouble juggling multiple projects and extracurricular activities. Your kid will be the same, right?

Or not. Placing assumptions on your child due to a one-word label—*gifted*—places you smack in the danger zone of unrealistic expectations. You know that no gifted child, including yours, is good at everything, but when that C in math comes home, do you remember this thought, or do you cringe, even a little, at this "low grade"? And, when your little angel gets lunch detention for "forgetting" to turn in her homework three days in a row, do you see this as simply a wake-up call for your daughter to get better organized, or are you afraid to show your face at parent conferences for fear that teachers will whisper, "Yes, those are the parents of the gifted girl who got detention!"?

The label itself should change virtually nothing about the expectations you have for you child, in and out of school. Why? Because the label seldom comes as a surprise, serving more as a validation of your suspicions than as brand new information. Too, the kid who had the label applied on September 19 is the same kid you tucked into bed on September 18. If he was goofy and disorganized and wore nonmatching socks before being identified as gifted, he's likely to be the same even after the aura of giftedness has been noted. Keeping your expectations in check and being realistic is a challenge. After all, when your 140 IQ kid forgets to take out the trash—again—it's natural to want to say, "Aren't you supposed to be gifted? How can you forget something so simple?" Stifle this temptation, as even if it's said in jest, it's just one more subtle indicator that gifted kids are supposed to be flawless, not real.

Issue #1B: The Aura of the Gifted Label (Student Perspective)

Your fifth grader is sitting in her mixed-ability social studies class and last week's quizzes on Bulgaria's prosperity are being returned. Your daughter earned a B, which is fine with her, as she is far more interested in emerging Asian economies than those of former Soviet republics. Still, the kid behind her—a competitive little thing—spies your daughter's B and whispers oh-so-coquettishly, "Hmmm . . . I got an A on the quiz, and I don't even go to that stupid gifted program."

Slam . . . dunk. One more small but significant indicator to your daughter that this gifted label is sometimes not all it's cracked up to be.

It is not uncommon for gifted kids to be reminded that they are supposed to act gifted 24/7/365. Classmates and teachers alike look incredulous if a gifted child answers a question incorrectly. Responsibility is an assumed trait, so it's not unusual that when a gifted child joins in on the armpit chorus when the substitute teacher asks for quiet, the real teacher returns the next day and says to all, "I am especially surprised that John (yes, your John) took part in this immature activity. I count on you to be a role model, John." Time and again it happens, in and out of school. Grandma gives your gifted child $5 for every A, but nothing for any other grade, while she rewards the nonidenti-

> Given these superinflated expectations for perfect grades, behavior and organization, it is no wonder that many gifted children feel, despite their efforts not to, that it is their job to be flawless.

fied sibling with $10 for every A and $5 for every B, because, "He has to work for his grades, dear. Yours come naturally."

Given these superinflated expectations for perfect grades, behavior, and organization, it is no wonder that many gifted children feel, despite their efforts not to, that it is their job to be flawless. Disappointment follows when any level of success lower than perfection is reached, so much so that many gifted students regard a B+ as the worst grade of all, "because I came so close, but still 'failed.'" Ouch.

Issue #2: Fear of the Future

I've been in enough classrooms in my life to know that many teachers—indeed, perhaps most—see the grade they are teaching as a dress rehearsal for something bigger in the real world. Whether it's 12th-grade English ("College is tough, you know") or 5th-grade fractions ("If you don't learn them now, you'll be behind next year"), teachers lead students to believe that the worst is yet to come.

Yet, as I reflect on my favorite teachers, I recall the ones who cared more about today than tomorrow. Mrs. Bradley made second grade special for me because we sang everyday in class, for no reason at all. Mr. Bennett, my first male teacher, extended our recess on warm, fall days so that he could teach both the boys and the girls how to throw a spiral and fake a pass. And, in 11th-grade American Government, Mr. Maloney played The Beatles' song, "Hey Jude," for our group of horny and vulnerable 16-year-old Catholic boys, informing us that the song's lyrics were not about drugs and sex, as we all thought, but dealt instead with something called "angst . . . a quality, gentlemen, from which you shall all someday suffer." I wrote *angst* down in my notebook so I would recognize it when it appeared in my life. Years later, when it did, I silently thanked Mr. Maloney for his long-ago guidance.

My point here is that when teachers or parents focus too much on the future at the expense of the present, education becomes a meaningless stepping-stone to a faraway greater good. I was never afraid to sing in Mrs. Bradley's class, and I don't recall her ever telling me that if I didn't learn "My County 'Tis of Thee," I'd be banished from third grade. And, at the time, I might have liked Mr. Bennett because extra recess meant less time for social studies, but I recall him now because he realized the importance of football and crisp, autumn days to a boy whose own dad was often too tired to toss a few laterals in the backyard. Instead of worrying about future events over which they had no control, these teachers concentrated on the "me" that existed that day. In doing so, I gained confidence to play around with this serious business called education.

As you look at your own son or daughter, stepping off the bus or out from behind the steering wheel, remember that the only assurance we have is that they are with us right now. We want their futures to be long and bright, and we do everything in our parental power to make that so, but if we focus so much on tentative tomorrows, we may be giving away the greatest gift we have—today.

Can you do at home what teachers sometimes forget to do at school? Leave the bright and successful futures that many gifted children have in their sights alone for a while, and remember to celebrate today's achievements and triumphs, and to put today's disappointments in proper perspective. Remember Bobby, whose note opened this chapter? His D- in seventh-grade algebra is not going to keep him out of Harvard; conversely, an A+ in seventh-grade algebra will not guarantee him a seat in that esteemed institution on the banks of the Charles River. Your child watches your attitude toward everyday successes and mistakes carefully. Tread cautiously if most of your remarks are punitive or psychologically threatening ("Do you *really* think these grades are high enough to get you into a *good* college?"), and pat yourself on the back if the encouragement you give is both genuine and good-natured ("I realize you are disappointed at not winning the spelling bee, but I truly appreciate the effort you took to succeed."). Simple, dumb things that state the obvious are simple, dumb things that really matter.

Issue #3: OK, Since We're Talking About Grades . . .

Carleton Kendrick, an alumnus who interviews potential Harvard students, meets with applicants on their home turf to see if they have what it takes to succeed in the "Ivies." Naturally and noticeably nervous, the applicants arrive at the interview to meet someone who simply wants to get to know them better. As Kendrick (2001) writes:

> I try to get beyond their Miss America-like, rehearsed responses. I'm looking for clues as to whether they'd make considerate roommates, inquisitive scholars and generous contributors to Harvard's community. Most often, these frightened, pressured high achievers have trouble finding their own voice. Instead, I hear them speak in the success-oriented words of their parents, teachers and college coaches. (p. 40)

Kendrick goes on to state that way too many straight-A students participate in organized sports at the last minute, "so it looks good on a transcript," or they complacently accept high grades instead of leveling with their teachers that the "new" material they are learning is old-hat. Or, they are fulfilling someone else's dreams, not their own. Sarah, her school's valedictorian, is one such example:

> "Math and science have always been easy for me. I don't like them nearly as much as literature, but they're what I do best. I guess I'll major in them in college, get a graduate degree in them and then get an engineering job and get married. That's what my parents expect." Sarah was 17, a broken sparrow, dying to be middle age. (Kendrick, 2001, p. 40)

Not long ago, Stanford University received 14,912 applications for its upcoming freshman class. Of these, 3,200 applicants had straight-A averages and the rest were not far behind. Yet, only 2,626 students were accepted, leaving disappointment—indeed, devastation—for thousands of top scholars who thought they had done the right thing by earning the highest of high GPAs. But, without a vision, without a passion to pursue one's own dreams—even if they are unrealistic and odd—these straight-A students were the academic equivalent of Stepford Wives, cookie-cutter copies of one another speaking in united monotone. Sorry . . . they're not Stanford material.

So, what to do? Of course, you already know the answer but, should it have slipped your mind, let me introduce you to E. Paul Torrance, an investigator of creative children and adults for more than 60 years, who will remind you of the obvious.

How To Grow Up Creatively Gifted

1. Don't be afraid to "fall in love" with something and pursue it with intensity. (You will do best what you like to do most.)
2. Know, understand, take pride in, practice, develop, use, exploit, and enjoy your greatest strengths.
3. Learn to free yourself from the expectations of others and to walk away from the games they try to impose on you.
4. Free yourself to "play your own game" in such a way as to make good use of your gifts.
5. Find a great teacher or mentor who will help you.
6. Don't waste a lot of expensive, unproductive energy trying to be well rounded. (Don't try to do everything; do what you can do well and what you love.)
7. Learn the skills of interdependence. (Learn to depend upon one another, giving freely of your greatest strengths and most intense loves.)

Note. Compiled from Torrance, Murdock, & Fletcher, 1996.

Post this chart someplace obvious, and highlight in bright yellow or pink those items that matter most to you. Write all over the page, and encourage your children to do the same. Discuss the meaning of these pearls of wisdom with your kids, and ask them, "What the heck do these have to do with being a 9- or 12- or 45-year-old smart person?" In other words, when school is over and grades are as irrelevant as hurricane insurance in North Dakota, consider what remains in one's life. You'll find, I believe, that Torrance and his colleagues hit the mark with uncanny accuracy.

Issue #4: Gifted Children as Political Pawns

Never before in our history have gifted children been exploited so blatantly. With today's mania for testing everything, year after year after year, to "prove" whether or not our public schools are any good, gifted children have been used to shore up academically weak schools. Time and again gifted children are told, explicitly or through implication, that it is *their* brains that will show government leaders that the neighborhood school is just as good as the private academy down the street. Because in today's world of providing vouchers for parents who choose to send their children to independent schools, every public school administrator is out to prove just who is the top dog when it comes to academic achievement. And, which kids will lead us there? You guessed it, yours.

This is exploitation for at least two reasons. First, because so much emphasis in our schools is to note competency, not excellence, the kids who score highest on mandated annual tests may, ironically, have learned the least that year. Second, due to increased pressure for all students to perform well on these assessments, many instructional hours are lost to test preparation; a "skill" that most gifted students mastered long ago.

Some high achieving students are taking matters into their own hands. In test-frantic Texas, Mia Kang, a straight-A freshman at MacArthur High School in San Antonio, boycotted the Texas Assessment of Knowledge and Skills (TAKS) test in 2005 by writing an essay on her answer sheet, stating how these tests are damaging her learning. The drill-and-kill mentality is destroying the thirst for knowledge and creativity in a whole generation of students, Mia contends, and teachers are forced to abandon lessons that deal with critical thinking, creativity, and discovery. Her school counselors admonished Mia, telling her she is choosing the wrong battle to fight and that she is jeopardizing her graduation. Mia's response? She believes colleges will see beyond the absurdity of today's politically charged academic benchmarks, and admit her based on her full academic record. And, if not, Mia has this to say, "If my high school diploma means I passed one test in the 11th grade, then that's pretty meaningless" (LaCoste-Caputto, 2005, p. 8A).

Just down I-35 and a bit to the east, Macario Guajardo, a fifth grader in Edinburg, TX, is also boycotting the TAKS, even though not taking it may mean he is retained in fifth grade, which is the reason for his refusal. With his father's support, Macario is bypassing the test because he believes that too much emphasis is placed on this one-time event without regard for the rest of a student's academic record (LaCoste-Caputto, 2005).

Did you just read right? Did I say "with his father's support"? Yes, and Mia also has her parents' support for her boycott. Perhaps there is a more important lesson than can ever be measured by the TAKS in these two stories: Families are united against the absurd premise and pressure that guides standardized testing in today's schools. If a bandwagon was ever needed to be joined in support of your gifted child's education, perhaps this test-taking boycott is just such an issue.

Issue #5: The Costs of Competition

What do academics, the school orchestra, soccer, and the science fair have in common? Each is competitive, whether the opponents you are trying to beat are classmates striving for a hard-to-get scholarship, First Chair in violin, the visiting team of athletes, or the seventh grader's trifold poster in the next booth revealing the secrets of DNA. Competition is imbedded in our culture in so many ways that it is difficult to come up with a group activity where the end result does not produce winners and losers.

To some people, all this competition is just fine. After all, in the adult world, we compete for jobs, prestige, and recognition. Whether it's the prettiest wife, the largest

SUV, or the greenest lawn in town, it is the rare capital-
ist who doesn't want just a little more, a little better, than
the Joneses next door. If we weren't a competitive society,
we'd turn off the Super Bowl when the Discovery Channel
offers an intriguing alternative.

But, what happens when the competition becomes the
goal in itself, rather than the happy result of striving to do
well? When even a silver medal in the Olympics is returned
out of shame of not winning the gold (this has happened), or
Nike sells millions of T-shirts bearing the message "Second
place is the first loser," we have lost sight of the original intent
of 99% of our competitions—to have fun, to improve skills
or knowledge, and to share camaraderie with others who
enjoy what we enjoy. In this climate of win or else, many
gifted children who fear the embarrassment of not being No.
1 opt out of the game. They sit on life's sidelines more out of
fear than disinterest.

Although it would be unrealistic to insulate our kids from everything competitive, we can attempt to balance these win/lose situations by doing simple things with our children that emphasize the importance of simply being who they are. For example, have you ever watched your daughter's eyes when you told her a story in which she is the hero? Do you recall the glow on

> Be silly together. Share mean-
> ingless secrets you promised
> to keep. . . . Tell them you are
> always proud to be their parent
> at a time when they least
> expect to hear it.

your son's face when you combed through the piggy bank
with him, looking for that 1948D penny that would complete
his entire set for that decade? Watch your teenager being taken
aback when you ask, "So what's your opinion on . . . " and
then you really listen to the answer.

Be silly together. Share meaningless secrets you promised
to keep. Send them a newspaper clipping at college about

an elementary school buddy who just got married. Put a happy face note in their lunchbox—daily! Wear Scooby Doo pajama bottoms (not in public). Admit when you are at fault. Tell them when you are feeling bad, and why. Back them up when they are committed to a cause, even if it's one you don't believe in. Tell them you are always proud to be their parent at a time when they least expect to hear it. Show up when you say you will, and stay away when you promised to do so. Have a race to see who can blow the most bubbles through a straw in a glass of chocolate milk.

OK, so this last one *is* competitive but, on balance, the others are not. And, that is the key word—balance—for when gifted children are put into competition because they are so smart, so capable, such strong leaders, they need to have downtime where they can do absolutely nothing except mess around. Or blow bubbles.

Now that I've revealed the issues surrounding expectations and why some gifted children feel compelled to be the best at everything they try, let's examine some of the ways that we, as parents, undercut our children's own efforts by saying things that are, well, just lame. They may actually sound good coming out of our mouths, and in our defense we will say that we stated them because we had the best interests of our children at heart. But, you know where that road leads that is paved with good intentions. So, with full knowledge that you might feel worse after reading this next section than better, I present four statements you should never say to your gifted child.

Lame Statement #1: "You're a smart child, but you are not working up to your potential."

The reason this statement tops the list of the all-time worst things we say to smart, underperforming kids is that it is so vague it gives absolutely no clue as to how to improve. *Potential* exists in the eye of the beholder, and there is no clear line of demarcation that separates meeting your potential and not meeting your potential. Certainly, grades are not good indicators, as many gifted children receive A's they didn't deserve (for they did little work to get them) and yet, may have struggled to attain a C in Latin IV. Which is worth more—the lazy A or the hard-earned C? Also, when we use the "potential" argument, we often do so with a certain smugness that turns kids off immediately. This smugness may not be obvious to you, but it is to them. Here's why: By stating "you are not working to your potential," there is an implicit message that we, the all-knowing and wise adults, realize what our kids' true potential is, and when they reach it, we'll tell them. Our game, our rules. But, if you think about it, do we really know the extent of our children's talents? Don't those limits change over time, as access to new information and interests causes our kids to achieve great things in some areas, but not others? Potential is a variable, not a constant, yet we treat it as if it were forever the same.

If you believe your gifted child can do better than present efforts show, why not say something like this, instead, "Simon, let's take a look at the work you'll be doing over the next 9 weeks in school. Which subject do you feel you can improve in, and how can I help you reach your goal?" Yes, it's still a sneaky way of kicking your kid's academic butt up a notch, but at least it focuses on specifics, not amorphous generalizations. And, specific goals are the only ones ever reached.

Lame Statement #2: "You did a great job, but . . ."

Everyone knows my Aunt Stella. She is like a motorist who causes an accident, but drives away oblivious to the mayhem left behind. Here is just one example of her poise. When I received my Ph.D. at age 28, I was the first in my extended family to get a doctorate. Upon receipt of my degree, my parents sponsored a party, Aunt Stella being one of the guests. As she drank her white zinfandel (ugh) and gobbled down the free food, she gave me the kind of praise Aunt Stella is known for.

"Jimmy," she said, "we are so proud of you. You have accomplished so much." She took a minute to chew . . . OK, two minutes. "Just one thing makes me sad," she added, "why didn't you become a *real* doctor? You always had the brains to become a *real* doctor." She shrugged her shoulders and squeezed my cheek, "But, we're still proud of you for this Ph.D.-thing."

If I had become a "real" doctor, I am convinced I would have gone into pediatrics. Aunt Stella's comments would have alluded to the fact that I had the brains to be a surgeon.

Your child has met Aunt Stella already—many times, perhaps. The world's Aunt Stella's are not cruel, they are merely misinformed. They believe they have the best interests of your gifted child at heart by always urging them to look ahead at what's next rather than examining what is good about what lays right in front of them. They second-guess every decision and every triumph, letting your child know that with a little more time, effort, or enthusiasm, they "coulda been a contenda."

That single word—but—is one of our language's natural depressants, dampening a compliment the way a rainstorm ruins a picnic. *But* diminishes the importance and worth of even the most genuine compliment that preceded it, erasing any semblance of pride a child might have accepted as credit for a job well done. In a very real way, it becomes a kick in the BUT.

The solutions are easy. First, tell your children that the reason they have two ears is so that some things that enter one of them can exit the other side without ever stopping in the middle to think about it. So, when an adult who really doesn't know your child (Aunt Stella never knew me, though she thought she did) gives them a kick in the "but," remind your son or daughter they have your permission to ignore them. This is not being impolite, but merely practical, for if every smart kid has to listen to every urge to improve from every person who thinks they have the right to offer an opinion, your gifted child will be inundated with confusion.

On the other hand, if the "but culprit" is you or someone near and dear to your child's existence, the solution is pretty simple—keep your mouth shut. Instead of saying "You did a fine job on that report, *but* if you had used five more references you might have gotten an A," simply say, "You did a fine job on that report." Period. End of sentence. Compliment stays intact. Should you feel strongly that you *still* need to prod your child to do better, that's fine. Just do so at a later time, after the glow of the compliment for a fine job has been absorbed.

Lame Statement #3: "This'll be easy for a smart kid like you."

Here's the scenario: Your child has decided to take an advanced class at school and you are very pleased, especially because the subject is calculus—your favorite! You know you will be able to help with homework in a meaningful way.

Class begins, and shortly thereafter, so do some problems. Where previous classes have been pretty easy, this one challenges your teenager, raising self-doubts about the wisdom of taking such a tough course.

"Time for me to intervene," you think. So you do. Dredging up your knowledge of things mathematical, you begin to help with homework. When your captive audience (i.e., your teenager) hits snag after snag, you watch the frustration and offer a word of advice. Hugging a now-slumping shoulder, you say, "I know this is new to you, but you can grasp it. In fact, in time this'll be easy for a smart kid like you."

Ah . . . I can already smell an argument brewing, probably beginning with, "Just because I'm smart it doesn't mean . . ."

Unintentionally, you just made a gifted kid feel dumb by suggesting a concept that was personally difficult to grasp is actually pretty easy. Your teen's inner thought becomes "Hey, if this stuff is so easy and I can't get it, I must be more stupid than I thought. Maybe I'll drop the class." It may have been inadvertent, but your words still sting, especially if your child was honestly trying to grasp an elusive concept that was crystal clear to you.

Instead of using the smart kid strategy, say something like this: "I can see you're having some difficulty understanding this concept. It is quite complicated. If it's OK with you, I hope that we can work on it together until you feel comfortable with it." This message validates your teen's efforts and acknowledges that calculus is difficult. Also, it indicates that even smart kids will have to struggle with new material sometimes, a situation that may be fairly rare in your child's prior educational experiences.

Lame Statement #4: "I don't care about your grades as long as you try your best."

Now, who could argue that this statement isn't a positive one? Well, me for one. Generally, this statement is said when a new academic venture is undertaken by a child who is unsure how well she will do. What happens, though, is a communication mix-up, as your child may misinterpret *your* best as *the* best. Further, if we venture into the realm of athletics, and we ask our child to "try your best" at water polo, the interpretation may be that best encompasses both academic and recreational activities. Doing something for the sake of just doing it doesn't seem to be an option.

Think of the unreality of always trying your best. For example, do you try your best at every element of your daily, adult life—in work, in completing household tasks, in exercising daily? Or, do you realize that it is sometimes okay to have a house that is 70% tidy or a four-day-a-week exercise schedule rather than a daily routine? By sending the message that high grades do not always count, but high efforts always do, you leave too little room for the inherent pleasure found in occasionally being average.

> By sending the message that high grades do not always count, but high efforts always do, you leave too little room for the inherent pleasure found in occasionally being average.

Trust me, as a mechanic I am mediocre. But, as an adult, I have the prerogative of saying those two magical words—hire out!—when faced with a task I do not want to exert my energy doing. Gifted children need the same degree of freedom to opt out of not being a top performer in everything they do. There is simply not enough time and energy in anyone's life to excel at everything.

Conclusion

Have I given enough examples of the many ways we go awry as parents when all we are trying to do is help? Do you feel the same sense of guilt reading this chapter that I did in writing it? Indeed, I could not have written this prose if I had not done and said many of the things I am now asking you to avoid. Live and learn.

As parents, there are many things we say or do that we wish we could take back later. We, like our kids, are imperfect beings, and it would be silly to believe that even our best-intended efforts are always interpreted in the positive manner with which we offer them. So, if you find yourself in these pages, don't feel guilty or dumb, just human.

And, should you think you've done irreparable harm to your gifted kid because you leaned too heavily on the achievement-at-all-costs mantra, just backpedal a little bit and be honest with your child: "Sam, I'm sorry what I said made you feel bad. That was not my intent. Let's go back and try again."

Life is filled with mistakes and miscalculations. What that means is that life is also filled with second chances. As we venture down this path with a goal toward being as close to the perfect parent as we can, let's understand how ludicrous that goal really is. It's the flaws that make us human and interesting.

In an odd sort of way, that's comforting.

Gifted Children Speak Out

"If I get a B on my report card, my world turns upside down and my parents go crazy. I told them to stop but they didn't, so I stopped doing homework for a while until they finally got my hint. Now, they're proud of whatever I get."

—Boy, age 13

"When I get anything less than perfect, it's like the world ended. No one else is that way. They can do anything and be happy. I do like the same TV shows, sometimes (That's not right, because I like the History Channel). But I do like the same guys. And I wear the same clothes. My hair is normal."

—Girl, age 15

"I have this advice for anyone who lacks self-confidence: Get involved in as many activities as possible. Not so many that you come to the point of being totally stressed, but to the point of where you don't limit your chances. Not only will you gain new experiences, but also you will meet new people, build new relationships, and find new ways to challenge yourself."

—Boy, age 17

Chapter 6

Living the Nuanced Life

n Chapter 2, I wrote about the difference between peers and agemates, contending that gifted children often find a natural affiliation with others who are older (or sometimes younger) than they. Fifteen-year-old Jackson knows well the relevance of this distinction:

> My mom swears that I am more of a child now than I was when I was a child! Now that everyone else is studying geology and reading *Mien Kampf* [sic], I much prefer watching Japanese anime, playing and creating video games, and talking about cars! I imagine part of the reason is that when I was younger I had no one else to interact with. The kids in second grade got sick and tired of me talking about and showing them my collection of rocks, and the kids in third grade weren't interested in why Hitler hated the Jews no matter how hard I tried to share

with them. Now, on the other hand, I have interests that coincide with people my age . . . video games, anime, cars, etc. I am never without someone to communicate with so there is little time to read books like I used to. It looks like I'm not doing anything "important" like I used to. But hey, I'm happy! (Personal e-mail correspondence, September 12, 2004)

What may appear to some as regression, Jackson sees as growth. An odd sort of equilibrium has been reached, where Jackson's intrigue with "normal" teenage interests makes him part of a group from which he was once excluded—agemates. Time, maturity, and perspective have softened the hard edges of this gifted child whose intelligence once separated him from other kids his age. Appreciating this social nuance, and being bright enough to recognize it as an asset, not a flaw, is vital to living a life that is not filled with disappointment or regret. The gifted child, adolescent, and adult share this in common—the desire to be smart and social simultaneously.

The nuances that exist in the life of a gifted individual are not limited to the social realm. The true measurement of success, the honest appraisal of one's philosophical or spiritual stance on life's biggest questions, and the fulfillment of one's own dreams and goals in a world where "great things are expected from a child as gifted as you," are essential aspects in a well-lived life. Also, they serve as great fodder for you, as a parent, to discuss something more important than grades with your child—the person they will become when you are no longer by their side to provide daily guidance.

Let's examine some of these nuances, but be warned, you may see yourself in some of these reflections, not just the child who brought you to read this book.

Nuance #1: The Myth of Underachievement

If I had not received a well-needed professional slap in the face from one of my students early in my teaching career, I'd probably now be selling shoes at some suburban mall. Only when I listened—really listened—to a gifted, but troubled, fifth grader in my special education classroom did I come to see the importance of nuance when the topic was school success.

Here's what happened. Matt was an 11-year-old who was very good at certain things: cussing like Chris Rock, irritating teachers to the point of tears, and revealing with obnoxious regularity that school had no personal meaning for him. I had the pleasure (note the sarcasm) of having Matt in my classroom for 4 hours a day. Four l-o-n-g hours. On those rare days when Matt was absent, my feet did the happy dance down to the attendance office.

Every day he was present, though, I gave Matt a menu of independent activities to complete in his study carrel—he valued his privacy, for he didn't want any of his classmates to see him "reading with the retardos" (. . . one of Matt's many charming appellations for my other students). Work that interested him, such as reading from a hunting magazine or completing logic puzzles that required complex problem solving to find solutions were done swiftly, completely, and well. However, the inevitable other parts of school—the drill-and-kill practice sheets I then used for spelling, grammar, and basic math—Matt did not complete. Instead, he would take a red crayon or marker and write a single word across the entire page—IRRELEVANT. He would then take these papers, ball them up, and throw them at me over the short wall of his carrel. Occasionally, for added flair, these "incomings" were delivered as paper airplanes. However they arrived, though, the message was always the same: When it came to educating Matt, I was missing the mark.

As a new teacher, I went back to the behavioral strategies my college education professors guaranteed me would work. I tried addressing the behavior, ignoring the behavior, making work contracts, detention, calling home, and going home (his, not mine!). Every one of them failed. My bag of tricks was empty, and it wasn't even November. So, I did what seemed a logical solution: I focused on my other students and tossed Matt aside as a malcontented nobody unworthy of my time. Now, he used most of class to sleep or read his own magazines. But, hey, at least he was quiet. I felt an occasional twinge of guilt, but since no other teachers were clamoring for Matt to be in their classes, I rode out that first year in relative peace and anonymity.

Our second year together wasn't quite as bad, as we just picked up in September where we had left off the previous June. But, I knew a truth that I was afraid to admit out loud—not only was Matt not doing his job, neither was I.

That all changed in March of that school year—late, but better late than never. On a typically cold New Hampshire morning, Matt entered the building, smiling broadly. A skunk had just sprayed him, and his silent stroll down the school's central corridor caught universal attention from students and teachers alike. They parted a path reminiscent of Moses at the Red Sea in *The Ten Commandments*, and Matt sauntered toward my classroom with all the confidence of Charlton Heston. He was in charge, and unafraid.

Immediately, we went back outside where Matt and I talked (downwind) as to the story behind the smell. Excitedly, Matt spoke as I had never heard him speak before, explaining that he was checking on the sugar maple trees in his backyard to see how much sap had flowed from the previous day. He then examined his buckets in his neighbors' yards (he had written contracts with them to tap their trees for a percentage of the "take"), and explained that he and his dad had built a stove to steam away the sap to make maple syrup, and that he was hoping to sell his product at our local grocery store once he was licensed to do so by the State Department of Agriculture. Until then, he went door-to-door with misspelled fliers advertising his sweet product. "Oh yeah," Matt added, "this is also mating season for skunks, and I got sprayed when I tried to watch."

There . . . did you catch it? My professional slap in the face? Delivered a year-and-a-half too late, it was still effective: Matt was a successful businessman the minute he left my classroom. This wake-up call demanded attention.

So, out of both desperation and a deep-seated desire to succeed with Matt that I had too-long ignored, I asked him if it would be OK with him if the remainder of his schoolwork this year be devoted to his business. Math would involve measurement, money, and temperature; language arts could combine with social studies as Matt and I would take photographs of the sugaring process. He would develop these slides, put them together as a show, complete with his own original script, and present this lesson to his fifth- and sixth-grade colleagues. For science, I found Matt a community mentor who was a licensed maple sugar farmer, who took Matt under his wing and showed him the ropes of improving the quality of his product.

Virtually immediately, Matt began to perform in my classroom. Those balled-up complaints about basic skill sheets were replaced with polite "Do I really have to do these?" questions, and Matt and I ended our too-long period of détente and were now talking and working as students and teachers are supposed to do—toward the common goal of learning.

The story is a long one, but because it effectively cemented my interest in working with highly able children who did not perform well in school, I thought its length appropriate. Here's why: From that day on, I began to see education from the perspective of the child who was receiving it, and I realized if I was ever to reach disaffected gifted kids, I was going to have to (excuse the pun) tap into their personal passions and talents.

Two years later, I entered my Ph.D. program, intrigued by this concept called underachievement. As I read the literature then, I had the same feeling about it as I read the literature today: a profound disappointment that we are way, way off course in both serving and respecting gifted children who choose not to perform in school. Indeed, in more cases than not, the reason underachievement exists in some of our gifted children is because we teach them to underachieve by asking for little more than blind devotion to a curriculum that is either too easy or, yes, irrelevant.

> Indeed, in more cases than not, the reason underachievement exists in some of our gifted children is because we teach them to underachieve by asking for little more than blind devotion to a curriculum that is either too easy or, yes, irrelevant.

Upsetting the Underachievement Applecart

Of course, most school personnel don't like to hear that they are, in part, the reason behind a gifted child's failure. However, if all that is provided to students is a one-size-fits-all curriculum, or if the one-day-a-week gifted pull-out program is thought to make up for the other 4 days where little is done to advance a gifted child's active mind, then indeed, we have met the enemy—and it *is* school!

My experiences have shown me that to use the term *underachievement*, and to apply the punitive and off-target "remedies" put forth by well-known gurus such of underachievement is to dismiss the gifted child's reality—school doesn't fit. I have even called for a change in terminology. Instead of calling a smart, low performing child an under-achiever (and I dare you to think of any positive spin you can weave with this word), I prefer to use the term *selective consumer*. For just like maple sugar Matt, virtually every underachiever has something going for him—a passion that drives him to pursue the intrigue of his always-active mind.

If you live with one of these selective consumers, see if the following traits look familiar:

- the ability to explain why schoolwork is not good or grades are low ("Look, if they'd offer something worthwhile, I'd learn it!");
- the ability to "read" a teacher in minutes, performing for those who give them strong content and high respect ("I like Ms. Cornelius—she's cool.");
- an independent intellectual streak that causes him to pursue interests with passion, sometimes to the exclusion of other obligations ("I know I haven't done my homework, but look at this new computer program I've designed!");
- has a strong sense of self and doesn't feel bad about low grades ("I could get high grades if I chose to, but what's the point?"); and
- improvement, when it comes, can occur overnight ("See? I told you I could do it!").

If these traits describe your "underachieving" gifted child, then the common guidance to take away their passions until they perform up to potential, or to put them on a contract so they know what they have to accomplish to earn a reward, or to remove them from the honors-level or advanced classes until they "prove" they belong in them will all backfire. Why?

The real problem—an unfulfilling school curriculum—is not being addressed. Only when the adults in charge take this child seriously will long-term improvements occur.

Here are some ways to address the very real concerns of smart, understimulated children:

- eliminate or reduce significantly any work already mastered;
- allow independent projects on topics of personal choice;
- place your child with teachers who understand and appreciate gifted kids' intelligence, humor, and sarcasm;
- incorporate problem-solving techniques instead of rote drill to learn or practice needed skills; and
- whenever possible, combine the typical school subjects of math, science, language arts, etc. so that students see the "big picture" of how these areas overlap in real-life situations.

Of course, when you first enter your child's school with these suggestions, you may be as welcome as a Twinkie salesman at a dentist's convention. You may be hit with comments like these:

- "If we do what you ask, we're simply buying into your daughter's inappropriate behaviors. When she starts to turn around, we'll consider what you ask." (In other words, no way.)
- "If we eliminate work your son knows how to do, other students will see that your son is getting away with not doing something they are required to do. That wouldn't be fair." (The fairness card is often pulled.)
- "In the 'real world' of work, your child will have to do things that aren't always exciting. Might as well get used

to it now." (In other words, the world is boring, so school should be, too.)

What should you do? Persevere, persevere, persevere. If a teacher or counselor who understands your point of view is willing to be an ally in your quest, receive this help with open arms. But, if you must go at it alone . . . well, then you must go at it alone. Know that your child is worth the effort you are making, and know, too, that the more often you can remind school personnel that you all share the common goal of success for your son or daughter, the more open-minded they may become. And then, if you reach Nirvana, and the school gates are opened wide to accommodate your ideas for reversing this pattern of so-called underachievement, have a major heart-to-heart with your daughter about her role in making this plan a success. Without effort on her part, the likelihood of returning to the "same-old, same-old," in terms of school requirements or structure, is inevitable.

> **What should you do? Persevere, persevere, persevere.**

Nuance #2: The Straw Dog of Gender Bias

I am the father of a son and the sole brother of a brother. How can these personal credentials possibly qualify me to write about and criticize (as I am about to do) both the work and the underlying premise of much of the gifted child education research that focuses on the specific needs of gifted girls?

I'll tell you why. After spending nearly three decades studying, working with, and writing about gifted children, I conclude that many of my colleagues whose stock in trade is the societal mistreatment of gifted females are guilty of the same sin they are maligning—pigeonholing gifted girls into corners predetermined by their gender.

You know the specifics, I'm sure: The pundits will tell you that gifted girls are less prone than their male counterparts to take advanced math and science courses in high school; that gifted girls learn by junior high school that in order to be popular they cannot also be perceived as too smart, or the boys won't like them; that gifted girls are supposed to juggle child care and their careers, while gifted boys can focus on their jobs alone; and that gifted girls avoid careers in technical fields so as to pursue options in the arts, humanities, or helping professions.

Yup, all gifted girls are clumped together into a conforming lot where individuality is assumed to be absent. Using literature from the 1940s–1960s to bolster their claims, authors such as Carolyn Callahan, Sally Reis, and Barbara Kerr lead us to believe that gifted girls are in peril while gifted boys have it made. The thing is, the underlying cultural expectations for both men and women have changed during the past 50 years. For better or worse, gender roles are fuzzier, and even though it is still more common for a man to be a geologist and a woman to be a teacher, no one scoffs at or looks askew when a female studies rocks and a male teaches sixth grade.

And, indeed, things in schools are changing. Girls now equal or outnumber boys in Advanced Placement courses, in both the humanities and the sciences. College enrollment is vastly overrepresented by females, and the percentage of males attending higher education is in decline at both the undergraduate and graduate levels. And, if you ask a middle school gifted girl if she dumbs herself down to look acceptable to the boys, she will likely look at you with puzzlement and say something like, "Hey, if my being smart is a problem for a guy, that doesn't say much about him."

Has it come to the point where gifted girls are having their dreams limited unintentionally by "experts" who remind them that life success and happiness are measured primarily by the selection of one's occupation? If a gifted girl opts to become a chemist, she should have every element at her disposal to help her reach that goal. However, if a gifted girl's heart lies in education, is she being made to feel less valuable by subliminal (but effective) messages with the underlying tone that "you're too smart to be a teacher"?

Perhaps this was never the intent of the research done on behalf of gifted girls; still, it seems to have become the result. My hunch is that much of the literature produced about gifted girls was written so that capable young women could keep their options open by selecting high school classes that are rigorous, leaving open many college majors that they would be denied access to without advanced math or science. Still, as I read between the lines of the gifted girls' literature, I note a definite bias, such as "Take calculus . . . it will serve you better than another elective in English." Pretty presumptuous, wouldn't you say, and especially intimidating advice for a gifted young woman with a passion for photojournalism over photosynthesis.

Anita Gurian (2001), in a publication about the lack of eminent women in our culture mentions numerous ways that parents and other educators can support gifted girls, including these:

- identify their gifts and talents before age 7,
- provide special programs that stimulate and challenge them,

- foster friendships with gifted peers who share similar interests,
- provide role models of women in traditional and non-traditional careers who have successfully integrated multiple aspects of their lives, and
- avoid having different expectations for girls than for boys.

My question is this, why are these same suggestions not equally as applicable for gifted boys as they are for gifted girls? Bias is bias, however it is dressed, and the fulfillment of one's personal dreams in life must be less a matter of gender and more an issue of personal choice.

A high profile career that is rooted in someone else's dream sustains an individual for only so long. But, when the adolescent dust settles and gifted young adults are left with themselves as the barometers of their personal worth, what a shame it will be if they look back on their careers with more regrets than rewards, realizing that they fulfilled someone else's goals, not their own.

So, as a parent of a gifted boy or girl, be supportive of his or her interests, whether these passions are quirky or typical, and expose him or her to the gender-neutral appreciation of the world around him or her. Advocate that your daughter take Tai Kwan Do and your son learn to cook. Bring both your sons and daughters to football games *and* ballets. Don't criticize your daughter's loud belching as unladylike while high-fiving your son on his booming burps. Let your daughter take out the trash while your son does the dishes. Small things add up, and if you react similarly to both your son and daughter who express a desire to become either an astronaut or a kindergarten teacher, then you will be breaking every stereotype the gifted girl experts would lead you to believe exist universally.

Nuance #3: Fulfillment Through Philosophy

When our son was 4 years old, he had a nighttime ritual that forestalled his bedtime by just a few minutes. As we tucked him in, he would inform us how many questions we had to answer before we could leave the bedroom and shut off the light. This good-natured routine was one we all enjoyed, as it put a comfortable capstone on the hectic day of a preschooler.

The questions were typically fanciful, like "If Batman and Superman got into a fight, who would win?," but on one particular night, one particular query stumped us. There would be two questions this evening, Matt told us, so, expecting a shorter session than usual, we asked for question No. 1. It was an easy answer ("No") to his request to paint his bedroom lime green, so it would look like The Hulk, his favorite superhero. Question No. 2 was quite different, "Do people feel the same way right before they are born as they do right after they die?" My wife and I gave one another "the eye," our typical way to indicate "OK . . . you take this one." Except neither of us wanted to take charge here. Finally, as Matt looked at us with a mélange of innocence and wisdom, I took a stab at this philosophical inquiry, "Matt, that's a very good question that people have been asking ever since . . . well, ever since people have been people! I don't know the answer, though, but if I find out, I'll tell you. Is that a deal?"

Twenty-three years later, Matt still awaits a response. So do we all.

I've often heard parents of gifted children talk about their kids as having old souls in young bodies. Not fully content until they have delved into topics that are imaginative, far-fetched, philosophical, and spiritual in nature, these children often probe the wonders of the universe that seem more appropriate for a college seminar than a playground sandbox. They want to know when life began. They want to know where God came from. They want to reconcile how it can be a crime to kill someone while most states allow the death penalty. They wonder what life would be like for them if they were born a poor child in Guatemala instead of a middle-class kid from Hoboken, and they want to know if there are such things as luck, fate, and whether or not our lives are "programmed" from the minute we're born. They fear death—their own and others—and they wonder what follows it.

As they announce these questions, often over dinner or while you are driving them home from soccer practice, you wonder, too. Except what *you* ask yourself is, "I wonder if I am I smart enough to be a good parent to a kid like this?" We don't want to lie to our kids, yet we also don't want to say "I don't know," so often that it makes us look incompetent. Unknowingly and innocently, gifted kids can intimidate their parents by merely being themselves.

So, it is good to know that recent work on bringing the big issues of life, death, and universal truth into a focus children can appreciate and absorb has begun. The study of philosophy, and the realms of wonder that it opens up to inquisitive, probing children, gives gifted kids and their parents common ground for investigating life's biggest mysteries.

David White's book, *Philosophy for Kids* (2001), begins with an overview of some ancient thinkers—Socrates, Seneca, Confucius—as well as some from more modern eras, like Rene Descartes and David Hume. He then looks at heroes from our time, such as Mother Teresa, Gandhi, and Martin Luther King, Jr., and explains in language that kids can understand, and parents will appreciate, how courageous people practice philosophy through their everyday actions. White then asks readers 40 questions that will help them put into perspective the down-to-Earth application of philosophical stances (e.g., "Can something logical not make sense?," "Can computers think?," and "Who are your friends?"). Is this book for every gifted kid? Not a chance. But, if you have a 10-year-old who is trying to unravel the mysteries of the universe while his classmates are still trying to master long division, this book is for you. And, never fear, even if you have never taken a philosophy course yourself, *Philosophy for Kids* will give you the tools you need to hold your own, even with your inquisitive 10-year-old gifted kid.

"When is violence necessary?," "What is a well-lived life?," and "When is it *not* better to tell the truth?" are just three of the questions you might encounter if you attend a meeting of the Socrates Café, sponsored by author Christopher Phillips. A former student of political philosophy, Christopher Phillips gave up his freelance writing career in 1996 to tour the country and give credence to the belief that it is OK to think about one's thinking. Many of his cafés are held in, you guessed it, coffee shops around the country, but others are held in libraries, schools, homeless shelters, and prisons. The usual participants are adults ages 25–66, but Phillips also holds these dialogs for children as young as 6 years old. At a recent event at Children's Hospital in Oakland, CA, when 10-year-old Mariela was asked "When is it good to lie?," she responded, "When you're trying to help somebody escape from something like slavery." This, of course, leads to the discussion, "What is slavery?" Like digging a hole in beach sand, as much as you shovel, there is always more underneath.

Phillips has published an illustrated children's book, *The Philosophers' Club* (2001), in which a group of bright elementary school students decide to start a "thinkers'

club" at school. The topics the children want answers to—
"Is it possible to be happy and sad at the same time?," "Why
do we ask questions?," and "Are the mind and the brain
the same thing?"—constitute the book's table of contents.
So, when you go to the chapter titled "What is silence?,"
these are the answers you are given: "What is noise?," "Can
some thoughts be completely silent?," "Is listening a kind
of silence?," and "What is the opposite of silence?" That's
right, no answers are provided, merely more questions to
probe the minds of young gifted kids whose thoughts are
seldom shallow.

A way I have brought my own gifted students into the
philosophical fold is to introduce quotes and their authors
to my middle school kids. Each quote relates in some way
to being gifted, and the task for the assignment is to find a
quote that "speaks to you" and elaborate on its connection
to being smart. Some of my favorite quotes are:

- "You have brains in your head. You have feet in
  your shoes. You can steer yourself any direction you
  choose."—Dr. Seuss (With so many paths to take as
  a smart kid, how do you know which one is best for
  you?)
- "You miss 100% of the shots you never take."—Wayne
  Gretsky (It is difficult to attempt something you might
  not do well, but are the consequences of *not* trying even
  bigger?)
- "No person is your friend who demands your silence or
  denies your right to grow."—Alice Walker (If it is not
  cool to be smart in your school, what price do you pay by
  acting average?)
- "When I was growing up, I always wanted to be somebody, but now I see that I should have been more specific."—Lily Tomlin (How do you know when you

reach your goal if you haven't specified what that goal looks like once it's achieved?)

- "Birds sing after a storm, why shouldn't we?"—Rose Kennedy (How do you handle life's inevitable setbacks and convince yourself to move forward?)
- "I don't know the key to success, but the key to failure is trying to please everybody."—Bill Cosby (How can you deal with people who aspire for you to do or be something not of interest to you?)
- "The respect of others' rights, is peace."—Benito Juarez (How do you defend to others your right to be educated at your level?)
- "The forest is magnificent, yet it contains no perfect trees."—Gye Fram (What role does perfection play in your life, and can perfectionism ever be justified as a healthy trait to have?)
- "The way in which my own life touches those of so many others, those I know and thousands of those I don't, has strengthened my belief that each human has his or her unique place in the ocean of existence."—Jane Goodall (What are the essential elements to a well-lived life?)

Quotation sites abound online (http://www.quote world.org is my favorite), providing you with an ample supply of pithy statements to mull over with your gifted child while eating a meal, watching a sunset, or walking on a beach. And, to take this an extra step further, have students read about the lives of Benito Juarez or Rose Kennedy or Alice Walker in an effort to discover the sources of their wisdom and strength.

Lastly, a way that I have engaged gifted kids in discussions of their own minds is to ask questions that I have long pondered about the high points and hassles of being smart.

I don't have one-size-fits-all answers to these questions, but that does not mean that these issues aren't important to probe. Issues like these can be discussed with gifted kids:

- How much information (e.g., test scores and IQ scores) should parents tell you about your intelligence?
- Who in our family do you think would have been identified as gifted at your age? Who would *not* have been identified, but probably should have been?
- Is there a circumstance under which you would choose *not* to earn an A, even though you could?
- Does having a mature mind make one more prone to stress?
- Is it possible to spend too much time alone? How might you know if this is the case?
- Under what circumstances, if any, is disobedience a virtue in a child or adolescent?
- How do you deal with adults who are your intellectual inferiors?

The beautiful thing about nuance is that it provides lots of intellectual wiggle room. Discussions in which mom or dad is simply a participant instead of a director or "know-it-all" are all too rare in our families, yet such interactions often lead to deeper relationships that transcend the roles we all assume in the family unit. Talking philosophy with your gifted child may seem like a big task but, as Robert Browning's famous saying goes, "what's a heaven for?"

Conclusion

Wouldn't it be a lot easier if our gifted kids came complete with instruction books upon their births? Owner's manuals for parents who want to sidestep the stumbles they assume they will make as they lead their able progeny through childhood, adolescence, and into adult independence. Of course, no such volume exists and, even if one did, I hope that no one would buy it. Today parenting is as it has always been—a learn-as-you-go exploration that has no precedent exactly like the situations facing you. Yes, some decisions are probably better than others in general (e.g., it would be hard to justify berating kids publicly in an effort to get them to succeed), but when it comes to the specifics of how to best respond to a gifted child's quest to know, or the sure-fire statement that will soothe the pang of being chastised by classmates for being "too smart to hang around with us," or the magical piece of encouragement that will cause your gifted daughter to pursue dreams that even she is unsure she can attain, there are no definitive responses and no guaranteed solutions that will work for every mom and dad. Instead, parents are left with nuance. The personal idiosyncrasies result naturally from the mixture of people and situations your gifted child confronts from day one.

> Today parenting is as it has always been—a learn-as-you-go exploration . . . there are no definitive responses and no guaranteed solutions that will work for every mom and dad.

As a parent, you will be neither flawless nor omniscient, but simply human. This path called parenting is carcassed with pitfalls and rocks, yet it is also lined with amazing opportunities to both teach and learn from your child. It all begins by recognizing that imperfection is as inevitable as tomorrow's sunrise and as pervasive as the bright-eyed excitement of a gifted child exploring another new horizon. Your prescription as a parent is defined loosely, but well: Be there with a helping hand and a shoulder to lean on; apply liberally, as needed. Repeat as necessary.

Gifted Children Speak Out

"I am more active in intellectual types of groups and clubs, and for that I am sneered at, called names and looked down at. But I try not to let it get me down because I know the other kids are just jealous, but somehow, this makes it difficult to participate in other activities at school (example: I am always picked last for a softball team in P.E.)."

—Girl, age 11

"School is ugh. Today in sociology we got into the topic of whether nurture or nature was responsible for development. What better way to teach us this . . . than to give us a worksheet! It gave an opinion on the nature argument and one on the nurture, and then asked us questions about our opinions. It had the same question phrased three different ways. I looked at it and got pissed. I don't know what to do. School is easy, but the way I am doing it isn't teaching me anything."

—Boy, age 18

"My classes are just too easy when it comes to giving us knowledge. We will go over Shay's Rebellion, but we won't discuss how the Rebellion set out a precedent for citizen political expression. We will discuss Sir Isaac Newton, but we will not examine how he influenced not only science, but also music, art, architecture and even literature. I am worried that I will never be stimulated intellectually until college. My older sister says 'it will get harder in high school,' but I am skeptical. When she says 'harder' she means 'more work,' not necessarily intellectually stimulating work."

—Boy, age 13

Chapter 7

Deep Roots, Long Branches: Using the Past to Understand the Present

John Wilmot, the Earl of Rochester from 1647–1680, wrote this about his life as a parent: "Before I was married, I had three theories about raising children. Now I have three children and no theories."

I'm not sure whether I am more comforted or chagrined that in the more than 300 years since John Wilmot penned those words nothing has changed! Sure, we have more tools at our disposal than in Wilmot's day. We have psychologists trained to help us understand our children and for them to understand themselves, we have books (like this one) that are intended to assist parents in raising their kids to be happy, fulfilled individuals, and we have pervasive online chat rooms just a mouse click away if we want first-hand advice from other parents confronting what we are facing. Still, all it takes is a quick walk through Wal-Mart where a toddler is screeching to get a "toy twuck," and his two, well-educated parents are at wit's end attempting to get the kid under control, to remind us of the wisdom of Wilmot's words. Such is the plight of parenting; just when you think you have it down, our kids act like kids, and we freeze like the proverbial deer in headlights.

> ... whether they were bratty or submissive, sneaky or out-front honest, ... parents would do themselves well to recall their own childhood antics.

The main reason this occurs, I believe, is that adults have forgotten what they were like as kids—whether they were bratty or submissive, sneaky or out-front honest ("Do you REALLY think brown shoes go with that black suit? Ewww . . ."), parents would do themselves well to recall their own childhood antics.

Then, when your gifted kid, who can talk her way out of any punishment due to her facility with words and logic, springs on you what you sprung on *your* parents, you can respond thusly, "I remember trying that line on my parents, Nicole. It's a good one, but it won't work on me."

But, I digress. The point of this chapter is to remind you that, when it comes to the similarities you share with your children intellectually, the apple doesn't fall far from the tree. Too, despite what you may think, parents of gifted kids often share the same intensities, personality traits, and unrealistic set of high expectations about their own lives as gifted children do about theirs. Yet, when we couple the word *gifted* with *adult*, eyes roll and denial is rampant. "I might have been gifted as a kid . . . " you will say, but out of fear that someone will think you are self-inflating your ego, you add quickly, "but I never think of myself that way anymore." Then, we change the topic quickly to take the focus off of us. The message we send to our gifted children?

"We want you to be proud of your giftedness, even as we are denying our own."

The Research Says . . .

I've long been leery of quantitative studies in education or psychology. Many seem designed to prove a point that the researcher probably held true before conducting the study, or research done with 25 people in a posh Midwestern suburb is assumed to apply to another 25 people living in squalor in an East St. Louis slum. Then there are the "well, duh!" studies such as those that show eating fast food daily will cause you to gain weight and have a lower self-concept (usually, it's the U.S. government that funds these types of studies). Let's just say that my jaded self finds that "educational research" can often be considered an oxymoron.

Some research does stand out, though, as irrefutable, such as evidence discovered from the time of Lewis Terman and Leta Hollingworth in the early 1900s that continues to be found today: Parents of gifted kids and their children have very similar IQs much of the time. Now, I realize that IQ does not tell the full story about giftedness, but it is the best that we have at our disposal for measuring the mind, so we can't discount it entirely. Accompanying these high IQs in adulthood are some characteristics and emotions that differ in degree from the general population—just as they do in your gifted children. And, it was none other than Annemarie Roeper who pinpointed a variety of these traits that link us to our children in ways we sometimes ignore or downplay.

Annemarie is averse to comparing people numerically. Instead, she looks at people over time—in her case, sometimes over decades—in order to fully comprehend their giftedness and the implications these high abilities may have on everyday life situations. Realist that she is, Annemarie sees giftedness in a way that should delight you:

> The greatest impact is actually made by the vast majority of the gifted whose light does not shine on the universe, but instead penetrates our daily lives. These are the gifted teachers, parents, cooks, bus drivers and letter writers. They are the quietly gifted—the privately gifted. Most often they're not aware of their giftedness. But the same characteristics are found in the privately gifted as in those whose contributions are better known. (Roeper, 1995, p. 94)

Annemarie then goes on to uncover 23 different characteristics of gifted adults she has seen impact their lives, all of which are listed on the following chart and some of which are elaborated on below. Her main point is this:

> Giftedness is an ongoing process and not a product. The process leads in a direction that differs from the direction of the majority, but which can also integrate with it and bring about change. It can lead to the greatest wretchedness and the highest ecstasy. The gifted person has the capacity to penetrate the complexities of the landscape of life and understand its supreme interconnectedness. Experiencing one's own giftedness—one's creative abilities—is one of the most exciting aspects of the gifted person's life. (p. 107)

As you read this passage, you probably thought about the gifted child you are raising. And, if truth be told, you probably understand that this statement applies equally to you, the parent.

Characteristics and Emotions of Gifted Adults

1. Gifted adults differ intellectually from others.
2. Gifted adults retain childlike emotions.
3. Gifted adults often feel fundamentally different about themselves than others feel about them.
4. Gifted adults are often driven by their giftedness.
5. Gifted adults may be overwhelmed by the pressure of their own creativity.
6. Gifted adults often have strong feelings encompassing many areas of life.
7. Gifted adults are not necessarily popular.
8. Gifted adults need solitude and time for contemplation and daydreaming.
9. Gifted adults search for meaning in both the inner world and the outer world.
10. Gifted adults often develop their own method of learning and grasping concepts.
11. Gifted adults have a special problem awareness.
12. Gifted adults are able to see patterns of development and growth, and therefore will recognize trends.
13. Gifted adults often react angrily to being subjected to public relations methods of image making.
14. Gifted adults are perfectionists.
15. Gifted adults are often confronted with the problem of having too many abilities in too many areas in which they would like to work, discover, and excel.
16. Gifted adults often have feelings of being misunderstood, of being outsiders, and of being unable to communicate.
17. Gifted adults have difficulty understanding the seemingly inconsistent and shortsighted behavior of others.
18. Gifted adults perceive a difference between justice and equality.

19. Gifted adults may find it more difficult than others to take risks because they realize more what is at stake.
20. One of the most outstanding features of gifted adults is their sense of humor.
21. Gifted adults develop emotional problems related to their abilities, but they also have greater resources for dealing with their problems.
22. Gifted adults often have difficulty with authority figures.
23. Many gifted people have strong moral convictions and try to use their specific talents, insights, and knowledge for the betterment of the world (Roeper, 1995, p. 93–108).

Let's examine several of the above statements in more depth, remaining conscious of the connection between the traits you see in your gifted child and those you see in yourself.

1. *Gifted adults differ intellectually from others.* More conceptual than piecemeal in their thinking, gifted adults grasp difficult concepts and phenomena that others struggle to decipher. Too, resentment can set in when you try to get others to see it your way (perhaps at work?), and you are told your ideas are too abstract, too expensive, too radical, too . . . everything.

2. *Gifted adults retain childlike emotions.* A delight in new discoveries or insights can make you giddy, and pains that others would brush off, you internalize to a deep degree. Dismissed as either naïve or immature, you are simply expressing the honest emotions that are a part of your being.

6. *Gifted adults may have strong feelings encompassing many areas of life.* When you hear about the intensities and overexcitabilities possessed by gifted individuals, two things come

to mind: first, you recognize that you could be the poster child for these traits, and second, you cringe at the realization that you have been "outted." Everything matters . . . and it matters that it matters.

9. *Gifted adults search for meaning in both the inner world and the outer world.* Making money and having a nice house is good—but not good enough. The gifted adult strives to construct a life full of purpose and is sometimes frustrated when others do not share this philanthropic vision of the possible. Through bettering the lives of others, this person becomes more whole.

16. *Gifted adults often have feelings of being misunderstood, of being outsiders, and of being unable to communicate.* Annemarie considers this situation to be the most difficult problem facing gifted individuals. In response, many gifted adults create in isolation—penning poetry they do not share or exploring esoteric hobbies that others just wouldn't understand. The result can be either enriching, lonely, or both.

18. *Gifted adults perceive a difference between justice and equality.* Too many people consider *equality* and *sameness* to be synonyms, but gifted people do not. Gifted adults can justify doling out different rewards for the same success or different punishments for the same crime; it will depend on the person and the circumstances. While others perceive this as inconsistency or favoritism, gifted adults merely see it as logical. As you might imagine, their favorite color is gray.

19. *Gifted adults may find it more difficult than others to take risks because they realize more what is at stake.* The risk might be physical, intellectual, or emotional and, before taking the plunge, gifted adults consider—sometimes overly so—the consequences of their behavior. As Annemarie writes, "it will take the gifted longer to decide to dive into the pool, but they will be less likely to hit their heads on the bottom" (1995, p. 106).

21. *Gifted adults can develop emotional problems related to their abilities, but they also have greater resources for dealing with their problems.* While gifted adults are often hardest on themselves when it comes to meeting self-set expectations, questioning whether they are really as smart as everyone says they are, they also have a greater capacity than others to step back and look at their situations rationally. Over time, this brings both comfort and satisfaction to them. Once their own worst enemies, they become their own best friends.

The knowledge of characteristics of gifted adults can bring the same sense of comfort Michael Piechowski's work on overexcitabilities does to people who possess them. Criticized as odd by people who do not understand that these traits are as natural a part of them as is their eye color or height, gifted adults learn to disguise or suppress the very traits that make them exceptional. And, if you happen to have lived life as a gifted child whose intensities were neither appreciated or tolerated, you may now, as a parent, try to shelter your gifted child from the isolation you may have felt growing up. This is a natural tendency, to protect those whom we love. Still, if you see your children exhibiting many of the traits and heightened emotions that are part-and-parcel of the gifted life, you need to discuss the beauty that can be derived from seeing in vivid clarity a world others see through limited, opaque lenses.

A Note About Depression

In reading the comments above, you may wonder if gifted children and adults who experience life in such a high emotional key are more prone to ailments and addictions than the general population. After all, if an individual feels as alone as Annemarie notes that they often do, isn't depression more likely to occur? And, if the world as it exists leaves you feeling hollow inside, isn't it preferable to carve out a new, artificial one with any manner of substances that create a new reality that is less bleak or more fanciful? Too, should all the drugs in the world fail to upgrade your self-image as someone who matters, does suicide become a viable option for the gifted, lonely person?

These issues have been researched some, but not much. Although there is no empirical evidence that gifted individuals are more likely to suffer from clinical depression or to abuse prescription or illegal drugs than the general population (Webb et. al, 2005), anecdotal evidence is abundant that being gifted does not make one immune from mental illness. Early on in the study of giftedness (or genius, as it was called way-back-when), a "scientist" named Lombroso thought that insanity and genius were bedfellows; based on this logic, every individual is born with a certain amount of brainpower that, once exhausted, leaves you a mental shell of the person you used to be. Therefore, since geniuses think quicker and stronger than others, they become insane in rather short order, as their "mind muscles" are spent.

Fortunately, when Lewis Terman came around in the 1920s, he determined that the 1,528 young people identified for his longitudinal study, *Genetic Studies of Genius,* were as mentally healthy, or more so, than the general population. This finding extended into the adult lives of Terman's subjects, crushing Lombroso's ideas into much pseudoscientific chalk dust. However, the legacy Terman left behind was mixed; now that he had shown gifted individuals were a fundamentally healthy lot, physically and emotionally, the impression was left that gifted people can act upon any crisis of confidence independent of others' assistance. In just one generation, gifted people went from being creatures of emotional fragility to paragons of mental health. Truth be told, neither extreme is accurate.

Today, remnants of both Terman's and Lombroso's ideas remain part of the mythological fabric about the make-up of gifted individuals. For just as there are some who consider the gifted "a little off . . . a little weird," there are others who contend that the gifted need no special assistance in school or life, because "they are so smart they can make it on their own." The first impression is leftover from the dark days of Lombroso, while the latter is a naïve interpretation of Terman's findings on the relative strength of gifted individuals' psyches.

The truth lies where it usually does—somewhere in the middle. So, just as I can state unequivocally that there is little evidence to prove that gifted individuals are more fragile than most when it comes to affairs of the heart and mind, I can also state unequivocally that there is little evidence that they are more able than others to handle life's emotional speed bumps without internal injuries.

However, when depression does occur in gifted children and adults, it is often colored in a slightly different shade than in the general population. Termed by some as "existential depression" (Webb, Meckstroth, & Tolan, 1982), it is a state of mind that arises from one's ability to contemplate issues about existence, while feeling impotent to affect change of any consequence. Tied in directly with the individual's personal qualities that make him gifted in the first place—the ability to think at higher levels, to make connections between disparate concepts and events, to envision a world that others his own age (or older) do not see—existential depression takes up residence in the child's soul; the internal loneliness is palpable, and often painful.

Existential depression may show itself in a number of ways:

- A pessimistic attitude about life that "the worst is yet to come." Every cloud has a lining, but it is not silver.
- Antisocial, negative behaviors that show up in sulkiness, aggression, rudeness, school conduct problems, and impatience with others. The true inner hurt is disguised by these outward displays, often misinterpreted as anger instead of elements of depression.
- A forlorn sense that one's life cannot make a difference in a world beset with problems that even intelligent people refuse to act upon.
- A feeling of being overwhelmed by the number of possibilities open to gifted individuals in terms of future occupations, resulting in a resignation that "I don't have enough time to do it all," causing a feeling of hollow success even with strong achievement.
- A feeling of rejection or separation from other children and adults who do not see the realities you do and, therefore, marginalize your anxieties as unimportant.

Existential depression does not occur just because a gifted person thinks about the bigness of life, the inequities obvious in a complex world of billions of people, or a pessimistic view of one's personal future or the status of our planet's health. When existential depression *does* begin to appear is when the gifted child or teen's views of reality are dismissed or demeaned by others. If the gifted child feels that there is no one to talk to, to share fears and solutions, or to simply cry out in anger or frustration, the seeds for existential depression are sown. This feeling of psychic isolation is bad enough when the child's classmates regard these concerns as trivial, but when adults react in ways that suggest a gifted child's grasp of reality is loose, that's when the trouble really begins. Gifted kids, in one way, expect their classmates to be clueless about the wider world; but when adults who are supposed to know better are oblivious to the very real concerns of the gifted child, then where is that child to turn? The answer? No place we want that kid to go.

So, what are you to do, as the parent of this type of gifted child? First, you need to take a breath and realize that your child is not saying what she is saying in order to scare you or get your attention. What she is sharing comes from a need to know that is simply a part of being able to see so clearly what others her age may not even perceive. Recheck those characteristics of gifted children and the qualities of gifted adults and you will note the source of this angst.

Second, be ready to listen. Do not provide pat answers that both you and your daughter know are lame and only meant to make her feel better. So, instead of saying, "I'm sure many people in our government are working on ways to eliminate childhood poverty," say this, "Sometimes, our government seems to have its priorities screwed up. Very few people your age realize this, but you see it clearly." A statement like this supports your child's view of reality and, if nothing else, continues the conversation for one more day.

Third, share any similar frustrations that you might have. A statement like, "I'd like to let you know about a situation that has been bothering me that I think you will understand. Can I tell it to you?" can open doors to communication that have previously been shut. Such a statement/request implies that you value your child's opinion. Even more, though, it shows a degree of trust and openness that is not a universal hallmark of parent-child relationships. Most importantly, it conveys an unspoken but vital message, "you are not alone in your frustrations."

Lastly, allow your child to propose a solution that might address even a small part of the issue being raised. At times, problems—be they global or personal—seem so big because the solutions to them seem so distant. But, even putting a tiny dent in energy depletion by walking to work one day a week, or saying to one friend who has dissed your ideas, "When you laughed at my concern about bullying at school, I felt hurt. I just wanted you to know that," may release some of the pressure built up by having no one to talk to but one's self.

Bottom line: You can take a mess and turn it into a message by opening the doors of communication with your children and letting them in on the little secret shared in this chapter about the needs gifted people continue to have into adulthood. These feelings of angst and uncertainty don't go away, even when repressed, and the questions gifted 5-year-olds contemplate about the universe and its mysteries are thoughts that gifted people never outgrow. Your presence along the way may not eliminate existential depression entirely, but it will put it into its proper perspective when it eventually does appear.

On Crossing Bridges Prematurely

Even though the end of each chapter in this book contains reflections from children about some aspect of growing up gifted, it seemed that the section above on gifted adults—you—needs a reality check that only a gifted young person can provide. So, I present Vamir, a 15-year-old on the cusp of adulthood in terms of chronological age, but already fully entrenched in one of adulthood's first rites of passage, freshman year of college. Concerned as much about getting dates as having a high GPA (" . . . college girls are rather reluctant to have a relationship with someone so young"), Vamir has a story to tell, questions to share, and wisdom beyond his years. Listen:

Throughout the years, I have found myself and my gifted classmates to be motivated, curious, creative and strong-willed (well . . . stubborn). In high school, especially, I noticed the independence of gifted students . . .

Here are some of my concerns as a "gifted student." I hate it when adults are condescending to me simply because of my age (if it's because I've done something stupid, it's my fault). . . . I hate it when I have so many thoughts that I lose one (which has happened to me at least a dozen times while writing this). I also hate it when I cannot think of anything, and when I have a really neat thought that I can't investigate more deeply because I just don't have the educational background.

I worry too much. I worry about "losing my talents." I worry about becoming average. I worry about my "lost childhood" and the opportunities I've missed because of my advancement (I skipped two grades). I worry I will burn out or overspecialize. I worry about how successful I will be in my career and whether my colleagues will accept me (and whether they do now).

Competition, standards and records I am striving for confuse me. Do I really want to do this? I cannot decide. Should I keep speeding up? The answer must be no, right? These questions make me doubt myself, my abilities, my sanity. It hurts.

About deciding on a career. Just like a little philosophy makes one an atheist while a lot makes you religious, a little knowledge makes you certain about your career, while more makes you uncertain once again. I have so many ideas for what to do and who to be.

I wish you luck as you grow up gifted. Always examine how you feel about school, learning, friends, and yourself. (Galbraith & Delisle, 1996, pp. 21–22)

There is an old expression that is supposed to give comfort and solace to those who ask life's biggest questions—we'll cross that bridge when we come to it. To gifted teenagers like Vamir, and to the young person on whose behalf you are reading this book, you need to recognize that crossing those bridges now, before they are even fully in sight, is a fundamental need of most highly intelligent people. Waiting until clarity is assured, and the bridge's length is fully exposed, just doesn't work for them. The need to share insights, wishes, dreams, discomforts, questions, and joys far overshadows the need to have definitive solutions to each of life's mysteries. Engage your gifted child and teen in intellectual conversations even if you fear that your arsenal of answers is insufficient to satisfy their curiosity. Taken together, this journey towards self-discovery may benefit you both.

The Gifted Adult as a Role Model

There is a common anxiety shared by many parents of gifted kids. Stated bluntly, it is this, "I'm not smart enough to raise my gifted child." Fearing the worst if you make a mistake, like not allowing your gifted 4-year-old to enter kindergarten early or, for that matter, allowing your child to enter early over the express objections of school personnel, you doubt every decision of consequence. You lose sleep over whether you did the right thing by forcing your son to take piano lessons that he'd rather avoid, or making your daughter join the peewee soccer league even though there is no denying that she is the Queen of Klutz. You may even avoid helping with homework or school projects, fearing that you will give the wrong answer or advice, resulting in a child who is scarred for life due to your intellectual oafishness.

My advice to you if you feel these anxieties? Get over it! Like every parent, you will eventually reach a point where helping your child with an assignment seems purposeless, as the content is either foreign to you or too complex. With gifted kids, though, this may occur in fifth or sixth grade, not in the college-level calculus class your daughter is taking in her senior year of high school.

> You are more approachable as a parent if you are not a know-it-all. . . . Imperfect role models are easier to emulate than perfect ones.

As parents, we are prepared for our children to outshine us academically, but when this takes place before the kids hit puberty, many parents of gifted kids seek cover behind closed doors in fear of hearing that intimidating question, "Mom, can you help me with this?"

The best way to address these anxious feelings is to let your gifted kids in on a secret—you don't know everything. Of course, when you share this truth, your kids will probably look at you with one of those "well, duh," glares, complete with eyes rolling upward. Hey, they have learned from past experience that even though you give them advice and guidance, they shouldn't always take either. They may humor you and say, "Thanks for your help," as they wend their way back to their homework, but don't assume that your words have a shelf life of any duration. If you've raised a polite child, he'll dismiss your inaccurate or inarticulate assistance quietly, rather then tell you that you're a know-nothing blowbag. And don't *ever* try to fake it and provide academic guidance in a subject you have not studied (or cared about) for the last 20 years. A simple "I don't have the answer to that" is preferable to a wrong answer in a subject in which you are not conversant.

The good thing is that your gifted kid probably doesn't care very much that you are not a walking, talking search engine with unfiltered answers to every query. Instead, they want to see you the way they see themselves—imperfect and vulnerable. Think of it—you are more approachable as a parent if you are not a know-it-all. Admitting that some topics are difficult or answers elusive validates your child's perception that life and learning are not cut and dried. Too, if you find a subject or issue difficult that they are also struggling with, this connects you in ways omniscience does not. You become more human when you share your ignorance about at least some things that exist in this complex world we all inhabit. Imperfect role models are easier to emulate than perfect ones.

But, simply saying "I don't know," to your gifted kids' questions does not get you off the hook. As a parent, you can provide a different type of guidance by doing something unexpected. Something like this:

- Sit down with your child (or by yourself) and do a little research that may help them to better answer their questions. Let your child's responsiveness to this assistance guide you; 10 minutes may be sufficient, or 2 hours may not be long enough.
- If you know someone conversant in a field of interest to your child, intervene on your kid's behalf and ask if she has any advice, knowledge, or resources that might be helpful. You could ask your child to do this, but your initiative in doing so sends a positive message that you heard your child's request and you took it upon yourself

to probe further into finding solutions you could not provide right away.

- There will be times when it is not the content of a child's task that is confusing as much as it is the scope of the project itself. An independent study on World War II is a bit, shall we say, daunting, without some specific parameters as to the focus of the study. Everything from D-Day planning, to Japanese internment camps, to the role Russia played in an Allied victory is worthy of a book unto itself. Your job? To help your child determine what bite-size pieces can be tackled first.

- Follow up. If your child asks for your assistance and you give what you know, wait a couple of days and ask how the project is going. If you were not able to be of much help directly, you can still show your support by inquiring about the status of the assignment. Or, when your child completes the project, ask her if she wants you to look it over, and if she would like you to check it for content, style, or clarity. Your role as a critic will be received better if your gifted kid has told you specifically what to look for as you read.

The role you play as a parent of a gifted child is complex beyond belief. Deciding to intervene only peripherally when the content gets tough or the issues complex makes you less and less of a focus of your child's attention. And, although some distance is natural and expected between parents and children, especially during the search for independence in early adolescence, the times when you are probably needed most are those when it appears your child wants you there the least. Can you be supportive, yet not obtrusive? Interested, but not cloying? Inquisitive, but not nosy? If you can answer "yes" to these questions, my guess is that the reason behind your success is that you communicate openly and often with that smart kid of yours who may be able to go at it alone, but whose journeys are more enriching if not every one of them is a solo mission.

Conclusion

It's something of a paradox, this thing called giftedness. As smart as they are, gifted kids can feel dumb when confronted by life's inevitable mistakes and challenges. As logical as they appear, they may be at the loosest of ends when trying to decipher how a long-standing friendship went awry. And, as multitalented as they might be, it becomes a struggle to hone in on those one or two areas that would satisfy their curiosity in a career or college major.

Parents of gifted kids, too, can seem rather contradictory. You want your gifted children to be proud of their abilities, but when they ask how you are gifted, you cringe and blush, and avoid the question more often than you answer it. You understand that giftedness encompasses heightened emotions and rich cognitive processing, yet when you register your feelings and intellect with full intensity, you look around to make sure no one is watching. You tell your kids it's OK to make mistakes, yet when you mess up in a big way, you do everything you can to clean it up before anyone else notices—after all, "a smart person like you should know better."

The intent of this chapter was to show you your own mirror image—the gifted child you are raising and how similar he or she is to you. Some parents of gifted kids will deny honestly that their children got their brains through genetics, but it is my hope that you will take a straightforward look at yourself to find that the intellectual and emotional overlap you share with your gifted children is real and strong. As a gifted adult, you need to acknowledge as real the similarities you have with your gifted children. Then, when the occasions arise and the conversations flow smoothly, talk about some of your hopes and anxieties with that son or daughter who is seeking the same answers you do about life's biggest questions. Finally, see yourself in a position that parents often play, yet seldom acknowledge: the emotional role model who may not have all the answers, but who is bowled over continually by the possibilities that lie ahead.

Gifted Children Speak Out

"There is some correlation between age and maturity, but not really all that much. Just as I am realizing that 16 is an artificial age of maturity that I have created for myself, the age of 18 or 21 is just as artificial. It is an expiration date that the government has placed on all our childhoods, and it is just as exact as those placed by the FDA. Nothing horrible will happen to toothpaste if it sits on the shelf too long, but the FDA has determined that there is a higher chance it will be ineffective if it is over such an age. The same strategy is used for determining the age of maturity, only in reverse. It is a horrible, inexact method of determining maturity, as book and moral learning are quite separate."

—Girl, age 15

"It wasn't until my senior year that I fell into a group of friends. Up until then, I'd been a loner. I was the 'class brain,' the one with the funny glasses and hair and weird clothes who never fit in, never went out, never got asked on dates. Then my English teacher pushed me to join the newspaper staff, and guess what? Everyone there was brainy, wore glasses, and had funny hair and unfashionable clothes. Even better, they all went out together, and suddenly, I was included in group parties and picnics and social events. None of us was popular in school, but we were all popular with each other. Each of us was a social misfit outside the newspaper office, but inside, we ruled!"

—Girl, age 19

"The worst part of being gifted is the loneliness. I am in a VERY small school in a rural area, and there aren't many other gifted kids around. I struggle with difficult issues like religion, morality, philosophy and politics, and there simply isn't anyone I can talk to. I have to deal with things all by myself. It makes me feel like I am very, very, very alone in the world. The best thing about being gifted is the level of complexity I can comprehend. I love hard concepts that make me reorganize my way of thinking. I think it takes normal people a lot longer to wrap their brains around those concepts, and I can do it faster. Sometimes, when the ideas are coming fast and heavy, it feels like my brain is dancing."

—Boy, age 17

Chapter 8

Write Your Dreams in Pencil

"Cheshire Puss," said Alice, "Would you tell me, please, which way I ought to go from here?"

"That depends a good deal on where you want to get to," said the Cat.

"I don't care much where—" said Alice.

"Then it doesn't matter which way you go," said the Cat.

"—so long as I get somewhere," Alice added as an explanation.

"Oh, you're sure to do that," said the Cat, "if only you walk long enough."

—Lewis Carroll, *Alice's Adventures in Wonderland*

Boulder, CO: Sun splashed vistas of the Flatirons; streams gurgling through the middle of town; "Trustafarians" (rich kids who dress like beggars) in tie-dye on Pearl Street;

Western ambiance at its finest. Oh yes, the University of Colorado. It's in Boulder, and is as beautiful a college campus as you will find anywhere. And, it was that university— CU—that our son, Matt, wanted to attend since he was 12 years old.

Knowing Matt as we do, we didn't argue, for at that age, he changed his mind about future matters as frequently as I changed my socks. We decided to humor his interest in CU, occasionally asking questions about why he wanted to attend there, what attracted him to a region of the country he had visited only twice, and what CU offered in terms of interesting majors that intrigued him. Matt's answer to any question about CU was always the same: "skiing."

Oh well, when you're 12 years old, I guess there could be worse reasons for wanting to leave home!

But, the yen never wavered. Year after year, Matt's fascination with this campus in the West increased. He watched every football game he could find on ESPN where the CU Buffaloes were involved, and each winter, Matt tallied the length of the ski season, the number of times I-70 was closed at Vail Pass, and the number of inches of snow that had fallen throughout the long, long winters. But, his interest grew into seriousness as he began to contemplate majors and, upon finding that they had his chosen field of film studies, Matt locked in with surety that he would soon be a Buffalo.

And, then it came time to apply to college. Knowing full well that his acceptance at CU was not assured, he did what any aspiring, optimistic teenager would do—he applied for early admission, informing us that he was not applying elsewhere.

"I'll get in," he told us with indomitable surety.

We gulped in fear that our son, a strong enough student with a good, though not stellar, high school record, would not land the dream he had chosen to target. The University of Colorado has high admission standards and receives applications from thousands of Buffalo wannabes from the flatlands who see Boulder as a cultural oasis, a bastion of intellectual growth, and a quick ride away from some of the world's best slaloms. Would Matt pass the muster and be seen by strangers in the same way we saw our son—an independent, focused, intelligent, and sensitive dreamer filled with passion and grit?

To make a long story short, CU said "yes"! As I came home that glorious day, with Matt sitting at the kitchen table among a pile of forms, he looked up and uttered seven words through tear-streaked eyes, "Dad, I'm going to be a Buffalo!"

His dream realized, the serious matters of choosing a dorm, applying for scholarships, and making plans for the big move West occupied Matt's full attention. As his parents, we just sat back and watched, awash in the glow of our son's excitement and proud of the sense of purpose that accompanied Matt's sense of discovery.

Arriving in Boulder in late August, Matt didn't even grit his teeth (we did) when we saw that his dorm room overlooked a dumpster, not the mountains. And he didn't seem alarmed (we did) when his roommate, a waif from Florida, was already on academic probation due to low grades during his required summer classes. Matt didn't even seem concerned (we did) when he learned that his survey class in chemistry would have more than 400 students in its lecture section—about half the size of his entire high school.

But ah . . . there were the mountains, and the promise of crisp, autumn afternoons at football games, classes that Matt would enjoy and be challenged in, and the chance to meet new friends amid a spectacular backdrop of nature's splendor. Also, if all else failed, some good friends of ours lived only 60 minutes away, where a home-cooked meal and familiar voices would gloss over any homesickness that might occur. The stage was set for a perfect melding of dream with reality.

    . . . Until this:

September 16

Dear Mom and Dad:

    At present, a desire to quell many of my anxieties, fears and stresses that reside inside of me causes me to write to you. During the past several days, I have found that I am continually contemplating the "what ifs" of my future. I know I am not alone in my fears, but still, that doesn't ease my worried mind. It seems that college and all that surrounds its demands are too overwhelming. I find myself studying continually, but still feeling that I am looking up a long ladder even after closing my textbooks. However, as I walk to and from class or the library, I see a large abundance of students enjoying themselves in the various courtyards and fields that the University grounds contain. As I watch and listen to the smiles and laughter coming from their direction, I ask myself what I am doing wrong to deny myself such luxuries and happiness.

    Another concern I have had in recent weeks is my longing to live in the past—the innocence and pleasure of childhood are thoughts I hope never escape my mind. I find myself remembering how much I enjoyed childhood, and I want above all else to be a third or fourth or sixth grader again. There is a strong feeling inside of me that the past hurried along too quickly and that the future is all too near. Does such thinking suggest that I have grown up? I would certainly hope not. Does such thinking raise questions of my maturity, my ability to adapt to change? I would like to think that most people, at similar points in their development, raise these same questions inside of their minds, as they struggle to survive during the darkness that haunts them each evening.

What can I do regarding all of these fears, anxieties and questions? I was hoping in writing to you that you could assure me that I am thinking "normally" as most people under stress think.

Love,
Matt

P.S. Please send money.

There . . . did you see it? The evaporation of a dream happening right in front of your eyes?

As parents, freshman year in college was the worst one we experienced with our son. Even daily talks did not help bridge the 1,200 mile gap that separated us, and as the fall semester passed, even the upcoming ski season didn't add spark to the unfocused disillusionment that, once present, never left our son's being. We couldn't wait for him to return home in December.

More talk ensued, and an "out" was given: Matt could return home for second semester, attend college locally, and look for new horizons from a more familiar setting. Matt would have none of this. Determined to eke out a positive experience (. . . and some "awesome skiing"), Matt returned to CU the following term with two missions—to enjoy his time there while looking for an alternate school for his sophomore year.

Though not easy by any means, Matt did manage to look more forward than back and, following a quiet summer of reflection and reunion with high school buddies, Matt embarked on yet another adventure, moving to Boston to attend Emerson College. Emerson was as different from CU as any two places could be. It had no campus to speak of (the city was its campus), only a handful of majors to study, and class sizes that allowed everyone to know everyone by the end of the first week. The orientation for transfer students like Matt was a whale-watching trip in the open Atlantic.

Within a week of arrival in Boston, the following arrived to our Ohio home:

September 9

Dear Mom and Dad:

It is my belief that with each passing moment in time, there is one individual who basks in a spotlight given only for himself: one person echoing the famous words of Lou Gehrig. Somehow, though, somehow the many moments of my past week in Boston have not seen a change in the spotlight—it's been me repeating that I am the luckiest man in the world.

Tomorrow's greeting of day brings with it the beginning of a new school year, a time of change, hope and wonder. As this evening's darkness beckons me to slumber, I rest knowing that there is no other place for me to be as happy, as optimistic, and as at ease as that of my current state, and the 'morrow's morning brings not solely a ray of sunshine for all to see, but a spotlight for me to walk in once again.

I truly thank each of you for all you have given me—friendship, love, care and opportunity—for these are the happiest days of my life. Thank you for sharing them with me.

My love and sincerity,
Matt

P.S. Please send money.

As parents, it is much easier to get a letter like this latter one than it is to receive the one from Colorado. During the time of this emotional upheaval with Matt, we were frequently at wit's end as to how to help, just as he was at wit's end in trying to articulate the source of his discomfort. In the 20/20 vision that accompanies retrospection, though, we did arrive at some things we did right, even if by chance:

- We listened to Matt and, instead of trying to take away his grief or dismiss it as simply growing pains, we let him know that he could call us whenever he needed to, even at 2 a.m. Even if all he had to talk about was his continued confusion, a voice from home could provide comfort.

- We didn't try to come to fast, artificial solutions, nor did we try to erase his anxieties by telling him to just keep so busy that he didn't have time to think about how sad he was.

- We reminded him that since he was little, he has had big thoughts to share and people with whom to share them. We gave him a task to find one adult who could serve as that sounding board, and he found her in one of his course instructors who took him under her wing. When he told us her name, we called her (Matt said it was OK), ever broadening the lines of communication.

- We let Matt be in charge of finding his own resolution to this dilemma, offering to help as soon as he asked us to do so. This gave him a sense of both power and purpose, as his actions were directed to problem solving, rather than simply festering about how sad he felt.

- When Matt arrived at a new choice for college, we asked only enough questions to express our interests. Our son had given much thought to the next stage of his growth, and the last thing he needed from us was a lot of questions that doubted the logic of his choices.

- Just like when Matt played soccer in elementary school, we stood on the sidelines and cheered on his triumphs.

Years later, with Matt now out of college and enjoying his life and career in his chosen field, we took time to talk about his Colorado experiences. Time had fuzzied (for him) the dire straits he was in at the time, and as we recounted our own fears and anxieties, he was surprised by their intensity. "I didn't know," he told us, "I just saw you as being there and being strong for me." Such is a parent's role, I guess, to be a calm port in a sea of testy waters.

The biggest lesson I took away from this incident that I now share with you, as well as with my students, is that when you write out your dreams, do so in pencil. If the dreams stay true, you can still read them in the rich, dark script in which they were written. However, if you need to change your dreams, it is much easier to erase pencil than pen. The remnants of what was to be are not so obvious, allowing you to move on with a clean, unencumbered slate that doesn't contain the residue of loss, defeat, or failure.

Goal Setting That Matters

Imagine going to the best buffet in Las Vegas, where food overflows in reckless excess, and being told upon entry that there are more than 100 selections to choose from, but that you are welcome to taste only one item. Take as much as you want of this single dish, but make sure to limit your choice to that one favorite food. Talk about an unappetizing situation, huh?

I often find that gifted children and teens (especially teens) find the same type of difficult choice as they maneuver through school and life that we would have in experiencing this buffet dilemma. What sports or musical instruments should they play, when each provides its own kind of release and fun? What books should they read among the many thousands that sound appealing enough to devour in a night? What career should they pursue when forensic science sounds as intriguing as archeology, as both involve digging around to find the truth? So many choices, so little time!

In addition to the difficulty of selecting "one special thing" that will make your life enjoyable and personally satisfying, there is a related dilemma—figuring out whether the goals you have set to achieve are actually your goals at all. Let me explain.

Gifted children are often better at attaining goals than they are at setting them. Being smart kids, many are able to accomplish tasks with little or no struggle. But, what is the source of this success? Did these able young people set out to pave their own paths, or did they merely take a stroll down a road whose destination was set by others? Straight A's are earned in courses that high school counselors chose for you. Varsity letters are awarded for accomplishments in areas where teachers or coaches encouraged your competition "because you are one of my strongest team members." Spelling bee ribbons are hung around the necks of winning fourth graders who succeeded, in part, because Cousin Sally drilled them with words every time she babysat. In other words, gifted children are often successful in achieving goals that have been laid out for them by others.

Is there anything wrong with this? Of course, otherwise I would not bring it up! The problem is that some gifted children—and by no means, *all* of them—have difficulty making their own, independent decisions about what life goals to pursue because someone else in charge has always made these choices for them. At times, this external nudge to pursue a goal is quite subtle, as in the teacher who sends home a note about how "wonderful" it will be if 9-year-old Julia would become the youngest student ever to take part in the school's Geography Bee, or the grandmother who cajoles Joey into playing the clarinet because "your grandfather always wanted to do it, but he never had *your* musical talents." Subtle but effective, the pressure to attain a goal in order to bring satisfaction to someone other than yourself is a common occurrence for lots of gifted kids. The end result can be a child who is not only dependent on praise for doing well, but is also reliant on others to lay out the goals in life worth pursuing.

So the problem is two-pronged, beginning with others setting out a gifted child's goals, followed by said child's inability to determine which of life's many goals are worth "tasting," and which are best left off one's plate. Further exacerbating this dilemma is the reality of what happens when one of the goals being pursued requires increased attention if it is to be realized. Few musicians become virtuosos by practicing here-and-there, whenever they get the urge. Few surgeons perfect their craft by scheduling their hospital rotations around their bowling league schedules. No, in order to excel, three things are needed: practice, practice, practice.

It's time, then, to sit down with your child and look at the specifics of effective goal setting. But, in doing so, don't forget to share these realities:

- *You can be good at something you don't enjoy doing.* So often, gifted children and teens are competent in many areas. So, it is natural to assume that a student with a 100% grade average after 10 years of math classes actually *likes* math—yet, that is just an assumption. Too, a student who can whiz around the ice and score goals with ease may like hockey, but not love it. Just because a person excels in an activity or subject does not imply that he wants to pursue it with intensity, but to the teachers, coaches, or parents who observe this excellence from nearby, it is a logical leap to assume that excellence brings ardor. It doesn't always, and it doesn't have to.

- *Anything worth doing . . . is worth doing poorly.* Gifted individuals grow so accustomed to doing many tasks without breaking an actual or intellectual sweat that the first setback, even a small one, can cause them to abandon any goal that is not attained upon first effort. For the gifted person who lives by the common (but erroneous) maxim that "anything worth doing is worth doing well," it is often believed that *doing well* arrives on one's first attempt. If it doesn't, then let's look elsewhere for satisfaction. However, if you can pursue a new area of interest with the idea that you are going to mess up, blow it big time, look like a fool, embarrass yourself as never before, or look stupid instead of smart, then you will no doubt have what it takes to win! "Anything worth doing is worth doing poorly" is a great attitude for attempting new endeavors, for there are often only two things that separate *poorly* from *well*, time and practice.

- *Some of the most worthwhile goals will be neither fully attained nor measurable.* If your goal is to become a better friend, how do you know when you get there? If your ambition is to make a positive difference in the world daily, will you stop trying to do so once your good deed for the day is done? If becoming rich and famous is important to you, when will you know you are rich, and will this richness be measured solely in dollars? Same with fame—are you talking the cover of *People* magazine famous, or famous in the eyes of a child for whom you are a personal hero? Not all goals are readily measurable, and the standards for success may differ as one gets closer to attaining one's goal. This is neither intrinsically good nor bad; it depends on the goal and the goal setter.

- *Not every goal is worth pursuing to its conclusion, yet take pride in its partial fulfillment.* I remember thinking how great it would be to be a member of the Appalachian Mountain Club's 4,000 Footer club, an informal collection of individuals who hiked to the summit of every one of the more than 40 mountain peaks in New England that rose more than 4,000 feet above sea level. At age 16, this goal was lofty; at age 19, it was reachable, as I was more than halfway there; at age 22, I got my first real job and the goal seemed less important; and by age 25, I had abandoned the goal, not out of defeat, but out of deference to other goals that were loftier in other ways. Was I a failure? By one measure, yes, as I am still 10 peaks shy of the 40. But, oh, the sights I saw along the way to the realization of this partially-fulfilled goal make me realize I was a winner with every peak conquered!

With these essential caveats in mind, it is time to sit down and list the specific goals *you* have for *yourself*. Yes, yourself. If you are going to help your gifted children consider their own ambitions, it's best if you have come up with a list of life goals for yourself. Here's a primer to get started:

1. *Be specific*: A goal stated loosely is a goal not attained. So, stating that you are going to "stop procrastinating" is not going to help you get there, while "when I know I have a project due, I will make a calendar to segment the work into 30 minute portions" is doable.

2. *Be realistic*: If you've never golfed in your life, then making a goal to break par within one month of taking lessons might be a tad ambitious (although you do get a gold star for following the previous guideline about being specific!). Perhaps you can hope to break par on three out of 18 holes—how's that for a start?

3. *Be reasonable*: You are more likely to attain a goal or two if you start off with a goal or two. Frequently, it is not the difficulty of goals that keep us from attaining them, it is the number of goals we have set that is unrealistic. Start small in number and build from there.

4. *Be prepared to compromise:* A goal you set in August may not matter as much next June, for a variety of reasons that life throws at you. Too, as you learn more about the goal you are trying to accomplish, you could become bored by it or feel that you have saturated the satisfaction you are getting from your pursuit. If so, it's time to move on.

5. *Be punctual:* Some goals will be more long-term than others, and some ambitions you have may be driven more by curiosity than passion. So, if you are thinking about writing that cookbook that you *know* is inside you, give yourself a timeline for when the chapter on "Decadent Desserts" will be written. If it's not written by your deadline, check out the reason—lack of time? lack of interest? lack of ideas? Be honest with yourself here, and either revise or relinquish this unmet goal.

6. *Be generous*: Share your goal list with a friend or a trusted confidant. First, this individual might help temper your goals by telling you if they seem too numerous or ambitious. Or, this person can serve as a great source of support as you make the kind of small progresses on your path to success that can be noticed more readily by an alert outsider than by yourself.

7. *Be good to yourself:* When you have reached a milestone, whether it is the loss of those first 10 pounds, or the grade of B on that killer midterm in macroeconomics, reward yourself with something sweet: a compliment to yourself, a night out, a firecracker salute in the backyard. Hey, if you don't applaud your achievements, who will?

If you take the time to collect your thoughts and write

down your own goal list to share with your child, it will set the tone for a great conversation and activity regarding his or her own ambitions, dreams, desires, and fears. Which means, of course, that there is one other guideline you must follow:

8. *Be there*: It's very lonely to set goals in isolation, to celebrate them in anonymity, or to backtrack off a misguided ambition in the company of no one. Negative self-talk, the kind that comes with not performing as well as we hoped and kicking ourselves silly (but silently) over our stupidity, is a destructive, cancerous thing that does no one any good. Sadly, many gifted children are good at this bad thing, so *be there* when they are disappointed by defeat or bewildered by the next steps to take. Too, when that goal has been reached, whether it is getting invited to at least one sleepover party during the school year or making the honor roll for two semesters in a row when that has never happened before, the celebration is always more rewarding when it is shared—especially if the person wallowing in your pride with you is someone who matters, like your mom or dad.

Get a Job!

I was sure from the day I started high school that I wanted to be an English teacher. All the way through college, I took as many English courses as I could and the bare minimum in all other subject areas. The summer before I was supposed to go to graduate school, I got a part-time job at a bank. I liked it so much that I never left. Now, five years later, I wish I knew more about math and economics. (Andrew, age 26, from Galbraith & Delisle, 1996, p. 90)

Some gifted kids have two belly buttons—the natural one that comes with the territory of being human, and an artificial one that you get when well-meaning relatives point their finger at your gut and say, "You're going to be a doctor, I just know it. You're going to be a doctor . . . you're going to be a doctor." Enough poking from enough fingers gives you that "novel navel" that is felt, if not seen.

Career selection is seldom easy, but for gifted children the choice of what to be as an adult is made more difficult due to a common affliction: *multipotentiality*. Defined loosely, multipotentiality is the ability to do many things well, due to advanced abilities, combined with an avid interest in pursuing many of these areas of strength. For decades, researchers at the University of Wisconsin studied the career paths of gifted youth. What they found, time after time, teen after teen, was that multipotentiality is both a blessing and a curse. The blessing part comes with being able to succeed at almost anything that you put your mind toward accomplishing. The curse aspect is that no matter what career path she has envisioned, the gifted youth keeps looking backward, over her shoulder, wondering what she is missing out on due to her rabid focus on her chosen career path. A common result is a gifted college student who flits from major to major in search of an occupational Holy Grail—the be-all-and-end-all profession that will be fulfilling financially, emotionally, and intellectually.

Although multipotentiality is real and can be aggravating to the point of diminishing one's spirit to pursue a specific career focus, gifted teens who suffer through it seldom get much sympathy at home or in school. Why not? Other adults who charted their own courses early on and are satisfied with their life choices see only the upside of multipotentiality. They may make silly statements like, "Gee, I wish I had *your* problem—being so smart that you have your pick of any career!" What these adults do not understand is that many gifted young adults want their careers to provide all-encompassing fulfillment. A good salary isn't sufficient to attain happiness, it merely ensures that the rut in which you find yourself can be lined with gold. Still, arising day after day to pursue a path that provides shallow satisfaction is not a gifted individual's vision of success. Despite comfortable outside trappings, the internal desire to become something more, something different, and something else is as annoying and constant as a poison ivy itch.

> ... arising day after day to pursue a path that provides shallow satisfaction is not a gifted individual's vision of success. ... the internal desire to become something more, something different, and something else is as annoying and constant as a poison ivy itch.

There are ways parents can help their gifted children deal constructively with multipotentiality. The first thing to do is to introduce your child to the concept from an early age. For example, if they become entranced with model airplane construction at age 7, followed quickly by equally avid love affairs with botany, French cooking, and architecture, congratulate your kids on being so diverse in their interests. Encourage them to explore each pursuit until they have filled themselves with enough facts and insights to satisfy their curiosity. Remind them that the world has so many things to learn, places to see, and people to meet that it may sometimes be frustrating to not have all the time in the world to explore everything and everyone that catches and sustains their interest.

Next, have them record their observations of the world around them. As a special gift for no occasion at all, buy your son or daughter a classy blank book that becomes his or her journal. Whether bound in leather or shiny, satin

ribbons, the journal becomes your child's personal reposi-
tory for memories of passions pursued and dreams unfurled.
Ask them to date each entry, and invite them to reread each
section several months after they write it. As time passes,
themes will likely occur, and your child's inclinations
toward the arts or sciences may become more pronounced.
When, years after the journal began, your kids puzzle over
which of thousands of careers fits them best, their journal
may provide direction. After all, if a child's first mention of
becoming a writer appeared at age 8, and it reemerges again
and again over the years, these innocent comments from a
bygone era may be pointing your child toward the inevitable direction of becoming a wordsmith.

Another vital way to deal directly with multipotentiality is to introduce your child to people who are engaged
professionally in careers that hold his interest. When he is a
preteen, this may be nothing more than a couple of hours
of shadowing the veterinarian to whom you bring Fido for
his annual ringworm suppository, or accompanying Uncle
Ralph on his big rig to deliver Popsicles to nearby Safeway
grocery stores. As your kids get a little older, the time
spent can be more frequent, organized, and focused, such
as a Saturday morning volunteer experience in a hospital,
hospice, bakery, or library. And, as the end of high school
approaches, see if there is a way to earn academic credit for
doing an internship during the school year or in the summer as a way to determine what fits and what doesn't in
terms of career possibilities.

As a result of these experiences, the best thing you can
hope for, as a parent, is not *selection* of a career, but rather,
direction toward several career options. I have long lectured,
often to deaf ears, on the benefit of entering college with
no major at all, keeping one's options entirely open until
the gifted young adult gets exposed to the array of oppor-

tunities any institution of higher learning offers. Sadly, too many gifted college students begin their freshman year convinced in the surety of their career direction, only to take an elective course in comparative religions or cultural geography and find their eyes opened, horizons broadened . . . and confusion rampant. Their best laid plans of becoming a dermatologist get derailed after reading Jack Kerouac or painting their first still life with acrylics. For the student with no declared major, such exposure to this myriad of life's possibilities is a refreshing reminder of how wide and broad the world really is. To the student convinced (. . . so she thought) of her 10-year-long dream of changing the world by becoming a cartographer, such exposure can be stifling, intimidating, and the source of both anger and frustration; sticking with one's dream when new "evidence" of a world beyond mapmaking is revealed to you can make you question the legitimacy of your own ideas.

So, should your child be unable to answer that age-old question asked of every child, "What do you want to be when you grow up?," congratulate him or her for leaving all options open, all possibilities within reach. At 12 or 16 or 18, is it too much to ask what that young person wants to *be* at 35 years old? Yes, it is.

And if They Don't Want to Go to College?

I can hear your defeated tone already: "I've failed as a parent!" *All* gifted kids are *supposed to* go to college, right? Isn't that their collective destiny? Their path to success, fame, and financial independence?

Well . . . no. As someone who has spent his life working with gifted young adults from middle school through college age, I have found that the best candidates for entering university life directly after high school are the on-beam, high achievers who have always lived by the dictum of "*when* I go to college" not "*if* I go to college." These young people are prepared, academically and emotionally, for a path that they have trod well in the past—classes, exams, books, and deadlines. Other than the usual pangs of homesickness and the occasional feeling of being overwhelmed by their workloads, these students navigate the college waters successfully. They are enrolled in higher education because it is their choice to be there; they don't need parents or older siblings to tell them the importance of a college degree, because they are convinced personally that they are exactly where they belong at this point in their lives.

Then there are the other kids, the ones who either do not go to college directly from high school or who do so only under duress. Whether these gifted students found success in high school or slid by with a GPA just high enough to graduate, they saw that first June morning of not having to get up for a 7:45 a.m. American Government class as a release from the binds that had tied them up for 13 years. The idea of returning to that same rigid schedule for 4 additional years of more-of-the-same is as painful to them as a tooth extraction without Novocain.

So, what do you do if you happen to be the parent of a gifted teenager who is not interested in the college route? First, realize that you need to hear your son or daughter's reasons for wishing to bypass this experience. Perhaps the career they are interested in pursuing is one that does not require a typical undergraduate degree. If it is more vocational or artistic in focus, a liberal arts school might be a bad fit from the start. Or, perhaps they have no clue what the future holds for them, but they don't think they'll find it on a campus littered with other 18-year-olds bent on becoming someone big. Maybe they are simply tired, and would like a year to do something other than study, like test their emerging adult wings in the world of work or community service. Whatever their reasons, these students need parents who realize that, in the eyes of the law, they are now dealing with a legal adult. Coax, cajole, and threaten at your own risk; none of these works, as each one has an undercoating of disrespect.

Inevitably, some parents will convince a reluctant matriculator to give college a shot for at least a year. This can work, if the student is open-minded enough to put aside any preconceived notions of what campus life will entail. Often, though, the reverse occurs. Whether done actively or unconsciously, some students who don't really want to be in college will undercut their own success by making every night a party. Away from home and the daily pressure of "Have you done your homework?" they abuse their newfound freedom in ways that only become obvious at midterm. With the threat of academic probation, these students often toss back the blame to you, the parent, with caustic, off-hand comments like, "See? I told you I wasn't college material." At this point, the damage has been done, your child's negative impressions of college have been realized. Having "wasted" the better part of a year and thousands of dollars, you become the bad guy and your child, the victim. This is *not* a place you want to go.

Instead, how about considering with your teens some alternatives to college? Ask them if they have plans for what they will do with their time instead of going to school. Because it is often easier to figure out what you *don't* want instead of what you *do* want, this may take some time and effort on your child's part. Call in any reinforcements you have—guidance counselors, personal counselors, trusted friends, or others who can offer options that are not college-based. It would be especially helpful to find someone who succeeded without going directly from high school to college; more than anyone else, this person will have credibility.

Next, be as excited about their college alternative as they are. The greatest alliances with our children are forged when we show genuine interest in something that is important to them. Maybe working full time at Old Navy while taking fashion design courses at a nearby center for the arts is not your idea of a year well-spent. But, if this is your child's plan, and she has articulated well why this is important to her, your support will show the level of trust you have in the kid you raised.

At some point, you will need to get to the sticky matter of money—where will it come from and how much of what your son or daughter earns (if any) will be returned to you to cover food, rent, utilities, and car expenses—you know, those adult annoyances that are a part of being independent. If your offspring has decided that now is a great time to move out, they will still need your help in terms of budgeting their expenses. If you have a strong-willed child (and how many gifted kids are *not* strong willed?), he may state unequivocally that he does not need your assistance. Take this as another sign that the young adult you have raised is taking yet one more step towards autonomy. Mention simply that you are there to discuss any issues that arise when it comes to matters financial. Leave it at that.

For all of your sakes, I hope that the decision to attend college or not is made long before the end of senior year in high school. The more time you all have to consider and explore other options, the less slapdash your decisions will be and the more likely success will be achieved. Junior year is not too early to begin discussing what life after high school will entail for your able adolescent and, just like anything else in life, the longer you have to get used to a decision you don't like, the less awful it seems.

Will your gifted son or daughter *ever* attend college? Much will depend on how his or her goals play out during this first year of independence from school. If she sees the need for specific courses that only higher education can provide, or if a trusted mentor with whom they work has convinced them of the benefit of such a choice, then higher education may, indeed, be in the picture. *This* time, though, your young adult offspring will be going out of personal volition, not a parental nudge. In the long run, this one year (or longer) of personal exploration may be exactly what is needed to focus a bright adolescent toward a career path that is both personally and fiscally sustaining.

Writer George Eliot once said, "It is never too late to be what you might have been." With gifted adolescents, whose minds are as active as they were when they were 6 years old, learning will continue to be a part of their everyday experience, whether they are enrolled in college, teaching snowboarding in Vail, or feeding downtrodden families at the local rescue mission. So, when times get tough, as a parent, remember the three essential P's of parenting teenagers:

- *Patience.* Not every gifted teenager's journey will end up at the same place at the same time. Eighteen is still young enough to take risks, make mistakes, and start over with a fresh set of goals. As Chapter 10 discusses, "Life is not a race to see who can get to the end the fastest."

- *Pride.* It takes guts for a gifted high school student to forego the obvious choice of college to embark on something exotic, quirky, or simply mundane. As much as this kink in the college plan may sting you initially, take pride in the fact that you have raised someone whose sense of independence allowed her to choose a separate course.

- *Persistence.* When the going gets tough, and your now-adult child begins to question the wisdom of his decisions, be the one person who does *not* say "I told you so." Realize that few healthy people make choices knowing they are bad choices, and fewer still enter a new phase of life hoping to fail at it. By being persistently there to listen, persistently there to give advice when asked, and persistently there with a nonjudgmental outlook that reveals an abiding trust in your child's decision-making abilities, you are providing a kind of sustenance that will allow your relationship to grow stronger with each passing year.

Stepping Back . . . Stepping Out

Fool that I am, I proposed a last-day-of-school writing lesson with a class of gifted eighth graders I had known for 2 years. They were in the mood for field day events, yearbook signings, and the tear-inducing end-of-year PowerPoint presentation that serves as our send off to the high school next door. But, troopers that they are, my students cut me just enough slack to let me intrude for 15 minutes on their last afternoon together as classmates. My assignment was simple: Think back on the past school year and answer two questions, "What gives you hope?" and "What gives you joy?"

The room grew silent—there's a first time for everything—as I distributed paper and pencils, awaiting their responses. Here are a few of the statements my eighth graders made:

It gives me hope . . .

- when I see a friend succeed in something I helped them learn

- when I think of my parents still being alive when I am an adult
- when I dream of my college football team raising the crystal football after being declared national champs
- when a very biased person changes their [*sic*] mind
- when I see my mother going through so much, and still being strong and never hanging her head in shame
- when I see that only a few girls have someone to dance with
- when my mother says "see you later," instead of "goodbye"
- when I see another meal is on the table

It gives me joy . . .

- when I make babies laugh
- when girls come up behind me and put their hands over my eyes and make me guess who it is
- when I finish a good book and see the world from the eyes of a character in it
- when I read Maya Angelou's poem, "Phenomenal Woman"
- when I hear preschoolers singing their ABCs
- when my brother gives me a ride to school happily, with no complaints
- when I wake up on a summer morning, greeted by the sun, and realize that this day has the potential to be the best one of my life

As the students read their responses out loud, their individual and collective voices grew stronger and richer. When the last item was read, a palpable energy infused the room; we were excited and exhausted simultaneously, and this tribute to ourselves and those who cared about us made us realize just how much we had learned this year, not just about academics, but also about ourselves.

"Write your dreams in pencil," I advised the students, "so when you need to change them, you can start with a clean slate all over again."

> Write your dreams in pencil ... so when you need to change them, you can start with a clean slate all over again.

I wished them well as I thought back to the time when I gave my son the same message years ago. And as they left our classroom for the final time minutes later, we shared hugs, high-fives and warm, embracing handshakes. It was time for them to move on, and with a helping hand from home, their journeys will take them down many roads that lead to some intriguing destinations.

Gifted Children Speak Out

"I want to dance in my old ballet class, play my clarinet, draw thousands of pictures (good ones), create beautiful pieces of woodwork, cook and sew for my children, decorate my home, be an astrophysicist, go to Mars, and understand all of my questions about life. That's not too much to ask, is it?

—Girl, age 17

"When I look for a career in my future, the clouds really thicken. There are so many things I'd like to do and be, and I'd like to try them all; where to start is the problem. I'd like to be a physical therapist, a foreign correspondent, a psychiatrist, an anthropologist, a linguist, a folk singer, an espionage agent, and a social worker."

—Girl, age 17

"Nothing is so simple for me that I can do a perfect job without effort, but nothing is so hard that I cannot do it. This is why it is so difficult to decide my place in the future. Many people wouldn't consider this much of a problem; but to me, this lack of one area to stand out in is a very grave problem, indeed."

—Boy, age 18

"Being gifted, I have a strong sense of future, because people are always telling me how well I will do in the future. My feelings fluctuate from a sense of responsibility for everything to a kind of 'leave me alone, quit pushing.'"

—Boy, age 16 (American Association for Gifted Children, 1978, p. 7)

Chapter 9

Make a Life, Not Just a Living

I was flying to yet another somewhere to give a talk about teaching and living with gifted kids. As usual, pen in hand, I scribbled comments on some papers prepared by my students. First, I tackled a few projects completed by my college undergraduates; later, I moved on to my eighth graders' essays about the historical character whom they most resembled in terms of motives and goals.

Seated beside me, expense spreadsheets in hand, was a gentleman a bit grayer than I, yet still my junior in years. As he tabulated and erased, tabulated and erased, a whirl of air exited his tired mouth. He was frustrated, I thought, and as unhappy computing his calculations as I was overjoyed by evaluating my students' prose.

Reacting without thinking, I pulled out a couple of pages of my students' writing. I chose Gwen's reflection on the life of Amelia Earhart and Tommy's piece on Dr. Richard Olney, a man who studied the causes of Lou

Gehrig's disease for 25 years before, ironically, contracting the disease himself. To Gwen and Tommy, these two people were personal heroes with whom they felt a close connection. Breaking my vow to never talk to the person sitting beside me on a flight, I turned to this jetlagged stranger and asked a simple question:

"Would you like to read what my eighth graders wrote about someone they admire?"

Patrick—that was his name—looked perplexed at this intrusion of the personal space barrier we had both erected. Caught off guard, he gave only a polite, "uh . . . sure," as he took the papers from my outstretched hand.

"Got any more of these?" Patrick asked after several minutes.

"Just about 80 of them," I replied.

Patrick smiled, took a quick gulp of his drink, and said something that reinforced what I already knew: "You're a lucky man."

For the remainder of the flight, Patrick and I read essay after essay. He'd often pick out a line or two that made him think or laugh, and show it to me as a proud parent might display the newest photo of his twins. Eventually, I invited him to make any comments he would like on the papers, telling him that 13-year-olds would enjoy hearing from someone other than their teacher about the power of their words.

As landing neared, he read faster, hoping to get as many papers completed as he could. His comments were rich with warranted praise and poignant assessments of the depth of spirit most students' essays displayed. Upon disembarking, I thanked Patrick for the help; he thanked me for the chance to do, in his words, "finally . . . something important."

It was obvious Patrick enjoyed the material trappings of success—an expensive suit, designer wristwatch, and a first-class plane ticket—but such luxuries, once attained, returned as little satisfaction as did completing his expense reports. Reading eighth graders' personal essays, though . . . now *there* was something that made a man richer.

Some of you might be asking what this diversion has to do with this book's content and message, but my guess is that most of you already catch my drift—to live a life of hollow achievements dries up even the most ardent of spirits. So, picking up here where Chapter 8 left off, Chapter 9 is going to focus on the importance of making a difference in the lives of others, even as one pursues the "American dream" of the big car, bigger house, and biggest bank account.

> . . . to live a life of hollow achievement dries up even the most ardent of spirits.

The Importance of Importance

Our deepest fear is not that we are inadequate. Our deepest fear is that we are powerful beyond measure. It is our light, not our darkness, that most frightens us. We ask ourselves, who am I to be brilliant, gorgeous, talented and fabulous? Actually, who are you *not* to be? Your playing small doesn't serve the world. There is nothing enlightening about shrinking so other people won't feel insecure around you . . . as we let our own light shine we unconsciously give other people permission to do the same. As we are liberated from our own fears, our presence automatically liberates others. (Williamson, 1992, chapter 7, section 3)

When Makenzie Snyder was 7 years old, she bugged her parents to buy her suitcases. Makenzie was not planning on going anywhere herself, but she had heard of other kids her age who were—children who were being removed from their biological families to be placed in temporary foster care. When social workers appeared for the emergency home removal, they often carried plastic garbage bags with them, so that the kids who needed to leave could toss a few clothes and toys into the bag. Makenzie found this wrong, as it is hard to have pride in yourself when your life's few precious possessions are tossed into a trash bag. The image created for Makenzie an unacceptable metaphor.

Dragging her parents to any yard sale she could locate in her Washington, DC, suburb, Makenzie purchased every used suitcase she could find. By the age of 8, with the help of her Brownie troop and classmates who sold lollipops to raise money, Makenzie had collected more than 1,000 suitcases, distributing all of them to social service agencies. Now, at age 14, Makenzie is the proud founder of a group called Children to Children, which has thus far provided foster kids with more than $850,000 in needed supplies— and thousands of suitcases. Her goal? To extend her program to other nations (*Teen People*, 2005).

What is it that caused Makenzie to see so vividly both a problem and a solution that adults did not consider? What part of her intellect was activated to such a degree that this cause became a passion? And, if you see this philanthropic gesture as something worthwhile to engender in your own children, where do you begin?

Teaching Gifted Kids to Care: Character Development in Action

Thomas Lickona, a champion of the character education movement, noted that our two goals as parents are to help our children become smart and to help them be good. Gifted kids, by virtue of intellects that rise higher and faster than their agemates, have the smart part down pat. The good part may not come as naturally, yet the opportunities are often there to expose our children to actions that they can do to help the world in big or small ways.

It is often remarked that gifted children are more aware of the world around them, and the baggage it often contains. They watch the evening news and cringe at the thought that yet another forest is being destroyed in the name of economic development, or they hear of the newest arrival of an exotic animal at the local zoo and they writhe in anger that a wild beast has been kidnapped from its natural habitat to be put on display for callous onlookers in search of a thrill. Or, their hearts break as they learn of a local family who has lost all they owned in a fire, including both pets and possessions. When they see instances of the world going awry, gifted kids often feel helpless to do anything to make a change, as they know in some uncanny way that change is long, difficult, and complicated.

When confronted with the realities of a world that is not always kind nor fair, gifted kids react with the same variety of responses that the rest of us do—some get angry, some get sad, some ignore what they sense, and some choose to make a difference. If your child falls into this last group, and is determined to patch even a small hole in life's fabric, you will be put in the uneasy position of having to help your child decide how to proceed. Why uneasy? Well, unless you are a social activist yourself, you might find yourself (via your child) unsure of what advice to give—who to talk to, how much to say, and what to do if her help is ignored. Much like a coach, you will need to stay on the sidelines as your son or daughter progresses down a path that can be carcassed with pitfalls, as the adults your child is trying to help or whose opinions they are trying to sway look at your 10-year-old as "just a kid," a young someone without power, still 8 years away from being able to vote. You want your child to succeed, of course, but you don't want to be so obtrusive as to take over his mission and make it your own. What to do?

Follow Makenzie's parents' lead: They drove her to yard sales to find suitcases, no doubt lending her (OK . . . giving her) some start-up funds to get her project up and running. Finding social service agencies and delivering suitcases to them certainly became part of their jobs as coaches, but the main thrust of Makenzie's work stayed Makenzie's work. The project that began as a small attempt to make a difference has blossomed into a program of national importance and impact.

Where to Begin

If you are looking for ways to help your child become more aware of the meaningfulness of even the smallest of kind acts done genuinely, you need search no further than the local newspaper. As both a teacher and a dad, I have done this often. In school, in fact, I began a program for fourth through sixth graders entitled "Project Person to Person," in which it became the task of a group of these bighearted volunteers to scour the *Cleveland Plain Dealer* newspaper and find people in our community who needed one of two things—help or a thank you. Here are some of the people we contacted:

- Brian, a man who had suffered a stroke at age 29, recovered partially from it, then had a second stroke when someone threw a rock through his car window, striking him in the head. Our students wrote cards and sent letters filled with hopeful wishes for a full recovery, followed 2 months later with a video that included bad karaoke renditions of our favorite winter holiday songs. Eventually, Brian contacted us with his own song—the most effective way he could communicate was by singing—and his wife and two young children visited our classroom several times, cementing a multiyear bond of hope between strangers.

- Matt is the oldest of four children in a family whose mom and dad were both killed in separate accidents, a year apart. News reports stated that Matt, a college junior with dreams of becoming a teacher, would have to drop out of college to get a job to support his three younger sisters. In a schoolwide project called "Links for Life," our students created and sold paper chains for 10 cents each, with the goal of "uniting" our school by encircling it with the recycled paper links that were purchased by grandparents, neighbors, and others who heard of our project. At an all-grades assembly 2 weeks later, Matt came to address our student body of 800, and to collect a check for more than $1,900.

- A high school in Nepal, where the library had been washed away in a typhoon, was in need of money to replace books that had been lost to the storm. Keeping in line with the theme of books, students collected their own used books and had a community sale at our school, raising more than $650 that was sent, via a local Peace Corps volunteer, to this Nepalese school. The letters and photographs we received from the principal and students were heartwarming, and the message that the custodian had to sleep in the library so that no one would "borrow" these treasured books during the off hours caused our students to see the true impact and importance of their actions.

- U.S. soldiers fighting a desert war on foreign soil need a touch of home, we thought, in their tents and barracks. So, students created muslin banners, hand decorated with wishes of good hope and thanks, and big enough to double as a sheet, if needed. The photos and e-mails returned to us from thousands of miles away gave proof to the students that, indeed, a touch of home is always appreciated.

Sadly, in today's school climate of raising student test scores at all costs, there will be those who criticize such projects as being superfluous to the learning process. But, one need only interview several of the children whose actions made a direct impact on the lives of another to see that the true measure of learning has little to do with texts and lots to do with *context*, learning as it occurs in the real world. You see, in order to appropriately respond to Brian, who suffered two strokes, students first had to learn what a stroke is and what its aftereffects are likely to be.

> But, one need only interview several of the children whose actions made a direct impact on the lives of another to see that the true measure of learning has little to do with texts and lots to do with *context*, learning as it occurs in the real world.

(Too, they had to hone their letter writing skills.)

In order to encircle our school with paper links, students had to determine the diameter of a link, the perimeter of the school, and figure out how many links it would take to complete our task.

(Looks a lot like math to me!)

Our students' idea of a library was a permanent structure with multiple rooms, rows and rows of books, and air-conditioned comfort. In Nepal, the library is a temporary building constructed out of any available materials, housing several hundred books, at most.

(Oh yeah, our fifth graders had to locate Nepal, learn of its cultures, history, topography, and climate, and understand what a typhoon really is.)

Many a student had a dad, brother, mom, or cousin who was stationed overseas for a year or more, fighting in a war that is very controversial. Still, "Support Our Troops" became the rallying cry, even if some students questioned the actions that sent them there.

("So, what gives in the Middle East? It seems like there have always been wars there." A sixth grader's observation, posed in innocence and with curiosity, led to much historical analysis of this volatile region of our world.)

You catch my drift, I'm sure: Character education, if done correctly, teaches gifted children much about this world that they are enmeshed in trying to decipher. Basic skills? There seems to me none more basic a skill than gaining some insights into the beauty and frailty of the human condition.

As a parent, there is no need for you to wait until schools come around once again to recognizing the importance of programs like "Project Person to Person" (which was eliminated, by the way, as it did not seem to address any particular academic standards our school district was trying to attain Shame on that district where, happily, I am no longer employed). Instead, find ways that you, as a family, can contribute to our world in ways that make your gifted children feel as if they have something to offer back to people they know, or those that they don't. As I recommended earlier, the local newspaper is the place to begin, but if your child is involved with organized activities—Boy or Girl Scouts, for example—or you have taken up a hammer for Habitat for Humanity, you already have access to multiple ways of helping.

In the April 2005 issue of *Teen People* (not my usual bedtime reading, but I made an exception in this case), the editors highlight 20 teenagers who will change the world—some celebrities, and others whose presence is quieter, but equally as substantial. Among the standouts are:

- Mischa Barton, 19, actress and fundraiser for the Women's Cancer Research Fund.
- Zach Bjornson-Hooper, 16, whose research on the water quality on airplanes has caused the Environmental Protection Agency to develop new regulations regarding water purity aloft.
- Raven-Symone, 19, singer and actress, who speaks to student groups on diabetes prevention, a disease suffered by many in her family.
- Alex Hill, 17, who learned from a Ugandan priest about the poor state of medical care in his African nation, and who has since raised more than $70,000 for medical care in that impoverished country, including the purchase of the first ambulance to serve 140,000 people in 62 villages.
- Diana DeGarmo, 17, *American Idol* superstar, who is a spokesperson for Wrigley's Greenup, a community improvement group that cleans up run-down areas in her native Georgia.
- William Dunckelman, 14, who started Project FAME (Fine Arts Motivating the Elderly), a project that provides art supplies, books, and CDs to nursing home residents in 35 states. He has thus far raised more than $155,000 for such supplies.

As stated so well by that gifted grandmother of mine, Annemarie Roeper:

Children need to live in a world that is relevant. They need to grow in an educational environment that prepares them to make sense of the real world and gives them the tools to change it. The difference is that gifted children know this and can articulate it, while others just accept it. (Roeper, 1995, p. 142)

Who among us has not met a 12-year-old who is "gifted in the heart," preternaturally aware of the scope of the issues that everyday people face, everyday? Who among us has not seen a gifted teenager angry at some arbitrary decision that reduces another individual's dignity or autonomy? Who among us has not comforted a gifted young person who saw vividly the dissonance between an adult's words and his or her actions? For the greatest reason of all—the preservation of hope—character education is a basic skill that can be taught from home. In today's complex world, learning to care is as important as learning to read.

"Being" Versus "Doing"

So much of what I detail in this chapter highlights the merits of gifted children's and teens' actions on behalf of others. These are beautiful, selfless acts that deserve our attention and merit, and I applaud any young person who endeavors to increase the world's quotient of beauty, tolerance, or kindness.

However, there are probably some of you reading this who do not see your child as being this self-starter, this enlightened entrepreneur with a fully developed social conscience. Does that imply your kid is a "moral slacker," a selfish ingrate whose favorite word is *me*? That is certainly not my intent, to compare gifted children on a scale of goodness—and it should not be your intent, either.

Here's why: Like the rest of us, gifted children come in all shapes and sizes when it comes to individual personality attributes. Some, like the teenagers mentioned in *Teen People*, are very vocal about their ambitions. Even if they don't say much, their actions speak volumes. Other gifted children, though, are more likely to while away the hours in search of self-understanding or personal enjoyment without much outward interest in making the world a better place. If you have one of these children, enjoy him for the qualities that best define him: fun, introspection, a quiet passion for learning, or a rabid interest in lacrosse.

Too often in our culture, gifted children have been regarded as our next generation's movers and shakers, and if I hear one more time that the reason we need gifted programs is because "these kids will be tomorrow's leaders," I think I'll toss my cookies. The proper rationale for offering appropriate school services to gifted children is because now, today, they have learning needs that are not addressed in grade level curriculum and, just as with any other child with a special learning need, these services should be delivered now, today.

Who knows? One day, not too long from now, a gifted kid may grow up to cure cancer—but then again, this cure might come from a team of talented scientists, some of whom we never classified as gifted. Or, the next great President, able to bridge the yawning and growing gap evident in our nation's populace, may be someone whose social savvy is combined with a political finesse that is as galvanizing as it is rare. Gifted? Who would care?

Doing gifted things and *being gifted* may or may not overlap. And although we acknowledge the "doers" because their talents are displayed so evidently or obviously, let us not do so at the expense of the "gifted beings" whose insights into self and others might be heightened to the point where, very quietly, they make differences in the lives of others by being a superb parent, a remarkable teacher, or a poet whose unpublished pieces are enclosed in greeting cards to friends in need of a boost.

Let us not confuse eminence with giftedness, for when we do, we eliminate as gifted those whose talents are more quiet and subtle than most; we eliminate a best friend who always has the right thing to say during the worst of times; and we eliminate children who wish only to absorb information for its own sake, to expand their minds or enhance their spirits. When we confuse eminence with giftedness, we ignore the fact that the true essence of giftedness is that intellectual and emotional agility to transcend the obvious.

Praise your gifted child when he does something that improves the lot of another's life, but also, hug your gifted child who comes to you with eyes wide open and says, "Dad, I just touched a tadpole for the first time. It was awesome!" Excitement in doing and excitement in being are two aspects of giftedness that are equally as important.

> When we confuse eminence with giftedness, we ignore the fact that the true essence of giftedness is that intellectual and emotional agility to transcend the obvious.

Gifted Grown Ups Speak Out

"In this world, I'm in the one percentile. I'm rich beyond most people's wildest dreams, and I'm happy beyond my wildest dreams. Sometimes I can still feel the fear. It's like, *how long is this going to last?* But I have the skills and the consciousness and the awareness now to move through that. When I quit my job as a credit analyst and stepped on that plane to Asia to become an importer of exotic rugs, I began a walk down a road that felt like my own. If my carpet business suddenly tails off, I'm still going to realize how lucky I am."

—Todd, 30ish, as quoted in GQ (Veis, 2005, p. 168)

"Dear Teachers:
I am the survivor of a concentration camp. My eyes saw what no man should witness—gas chambers built by learned engineers, children poisoned by educated physicians, infants killed by trained nurses, women and babies shot and burned by high school and college students. So I am suspicious of education.

My request is: help your students become humane. Your efforts must never produce learned monsters, skilled psychopaths, educated Eichmanns. Reading, writing, arithmetic are important only if they serve to make our children more humane."

—A school principal who survived a concentration camp

"I stayed home with my children because that nurturing is more important than 20 years of medical practice. I am raising the future mothers of America, and that will outlast me for many generations. I need to be home with my gifted daughters to give them the special opportunities they require. My kitchen is a mess because they need to glue and cut and create things . . . I enjoy being there for the new idea, when they are excited and want to share—a caretaker could not provide that feeling which adds to self-worth. I would like to make them each a rock inside, very secure. When you have that inner security, you can deal with the world's unkindness."

—Theresa, pediatrician, quoted in Gifted Grown Ups
(Streznewski, 1999, p. 54).

Chapter 10

Life Is Not a Race to See Who Can Get to the End the Fastest

I n the movie The Incredibles, *Dash, a third-grade superstar of speed, is forbidden from participating in track meets because . . . well, he is simply too fast. He'll leave the competition (and his teammates) in the dust, deflating their fragile egos as they come face-to-face with their own limitations as runners.*

Mr. Incredible, Dash's dad, realizes that his son is being penalized for his talents and complains loudly about America's love affair with mediocrity. It's OK for kids to be good, but not so good that it makes other kids look bad.

In the end, Dash is allowed to race, but is reminded to tone down his excess speed—after all, no need to make others look bad in front of their friends and supporters.

How often does the above scenario need to take place, in various forms and contexts, before people realize that gifted children seldom have an agenda to make other people look stupid? When gifted kids perform at levels that capitalize on their strengths or talents, they are simply being who they are. To repress what they know, or what they can do, sends a clear message that excellence must be tempered with modesty. It's OK to be good, but being *too good* is bad. Real bad.

"Everyone's special, Dash," says his sister, in an attempt to mollify his disdain for not being able to display his talents fully.
"Which is another way of saying no one is," Dash responds, strongly, yet dejectedly. (Walker & Bird, 2004)

In this final chapter, I will attempt to walk a fine line between defending the right to be excellent while maintaining an attitude that not everything in life must be a race to the finish line. It is often a constant battle waged between gifted kids and their parents, gifted kids and their classmates, and gifted kids and themselves, to find that elusive balance between competition and collaboration.

In Praise of Elitism

When I entered the field of gifted child education almost 30 years ago, I was like a dry sponge, I lapped up every available bead of information about gifted children, absorbing every drop of knowledge indiscriminately, noticing neither inherent conflicts in logic nor opinions that went askew to my own beliefs. As time progressed and my knowledge and experiences deepened, I began to question and challenge everything. Like the gifted kid I once was, and the gifted adult I had grown to become, I searched my soul for the meaning and purpose behind my studies. Our field of gifted child education, though small, was filled with contradictions, as some individuals were "stingy" about defining giftedness, leaving it to those who had IQs so high that they would qualify as geniuses, while others opened the floodgates of giftedness to anyone who had an observable talent that exceeded what might be expected for a kid of a certain age. Too, some authors wrote about giftedness from the academic point of view, seeing giftedness as a school-based phenomenon, while others spoke eloquently of the emotional distinctions that permeated the hearts of gifted people.

So which was it? The stingy definition or the floodgate one? Academic achievement or emotional intensities? The questions constantly plagued me. They still do. In fact, the longer I study gifted people and those who teach and raise them, the more confused I become about the precision of my beliefs. So, when I decide on a satisfactory definition of giftedness that seems to fit what I've seen across legions of gifted kids and adults, I then confront a youngster who doesn't fit this mold, but still appears to be gifted. Hmmm. Or, even though I believe it is essential that gifted kids have opportunities to get together in school as the intellectual and emotional peers that they are, I question if bunching them together for too much time will give them an artificial view of the world they share with nongifted others. So, where is the supposed happy medium? And, will one gifted child's happy medium be another gifted child's academic purgatory? You think after nearly three decades of mulling over this stuff, the answers would be clear. Not so.

One thing that I have confronted honestly, though, is my comfort with the term *elitism*. You read it right—comfort, not discomfort. A little explanation . . .

If you've been interested in this field for more than 10 minutes, you will have experienced a gifted naysayer of

The Incredibles mindset. Believing that everyone is gifted at something, they pooh-pooh the notion of giftedness as a distinct quality that some have and others do not have. If all else fails in trying to convince you of their point of view, they pull out their secret weapon from the arsenal of terms that sends shivers up the spine of anyone who lives in a democracy, *elitism*. By singling out some children as gifted, you will be told, you are downgrading the personal worth of anyone who doesn't meet your high, high standard.

. . . To which I'd respond, "horsefeathers."

Now, if by elitism you think I advocate that gifted children and adults are somehow inherently worth more than those to whom this label is not ascribed, then you have it all wrong. The brand of elitism that pegs some races or classes of people as being superior to others is absurd and offensive; such beliefs hold no place in my personal repertoire. However, if it is elitist to believe in the sanctity of human differences and to state unequivocally that an IQ of 145 *does* earmark a 10-year-old child as different from other fourth graders in some important ways, then elitist I am. If it is elitist to take a child aside and tell her that her giftedness is a lifelong quality that will allow her to experience and interpret life situations in ways that are more sophisticated and complex than many, then I will proudly wear the label. If gifted students need a foot soldier to champion their rights to express their talents fully without fear of retribution from others, or if they need someone to explain that their emotional and intellectual abilities may make them stand out from classmates in ways that require a change in curriculum or grade placement, then I will be their man.

As always, our world and our homes need the richness of spirit and compassion that gifted children provide.

To abandon them to *The Incredibles* logic is to champion equity and excellence for all, making our gifted children sacrificial lambs on the altar of egalitarianism. Gifted children deserve better, and who else to take up the challenge than a bunch of elitists who realize and will accentuate an essential truth, that gifted children do exist, as they always have and always will, and to discount their presence and prominence in our world is to be the ultimate intellectual snob who would rather deny reality than face it.

Elitist? You bet I am . . . and proud of it.

On the Other Hand . . .

Similar to the law of physics that states that for every action there will be an equal and opposite reaction, the same logic applies when considering the uniqueness of each and every gifted child. For as individualistic as they are, with needs and quirks that mark them as unique even in relation to other gifted children, they also share many commonalities with other kids their age. This is the underlying reason that many gifted advocates, myself included, espouse the mantra that gifted children are children first, and gifted second. This statement in no way denigrates the importance of giftedness and its impact on many facets of the child's life. Instead, it legitimizes our common humanity. Consider this: Tiger Woods is a superb golfer, yet he is also a son who admires his father greatly and openly. Katie Couric is the queen of the morning airwaves, yet she is also a widow raising two young

> . . . gifted children do exist, as they always have and always will, and to discount their presence and prominence in our world is to be the ultimate intellectual snob who would rather deny reality than face it.

children. Barbara Bush is the outspoken wife of a former President, yet she is also a doting grandmother whose eyes light up whenever she talks about the antics of the Bush scions.

If *famous* people can have lives beyond the roles they play in public, our gifted children need to be allowed this same courtesy. So, if your son just came in first in the countywide writing contest, or your daughter is a finalist for a Westinghouse Scholarship, applaud these achievements until your hands blister, and then remind your child that the dishes still need to be put away and the toys strewn across the living room floor still need to be picked up.

This is such common sense, isn't it? Yet, when Mark Twain remarked that common sense is not so common, he could easily have been addressing parents of gifted kids who get so hung up on their child's differences from other kids that they forget to notice the many similarities they share—the need to belong, the desire for downtime, the temptation to experiment with adult sensations before they are ready to do so.

One gifted teenager addressed these concerns in the classic book, *On Being Gifted*, a volume in which 20 gifted teens wrote about the ups and downs of being them. This excerpt, a typical passage, addresses the desire for social recognition from agemates:

> Some people are turned off by the amount of recognition I've had; some people assume I'm conceited and untouchable, or impossible to get along with. *They've heard of me but they don't know me in person; they've read the reviews and think they've read the book.* People are prone to jump to conclusions about me solely because of any "gifted" image I may have; some people have already made up their minds about me or think I could never be inter-

ested in their more mundane things like parties and girls.

> On the whole, though, I have to confess that I'd rather be a troubled "genius" and a "struggling young writer" than a straight-C student who spends free weekends carrying bags at the A & P. (italics in original, American Association for Gifted Children, 1978, p. 20)

This young man's desire to fit in is fleeting, while his desire to maintain the integrity of his own uniqueness has staying power. Once he traverses the social minefield that adolescence can be, his sense of personal comfort with his high abilities will surely carry him into an adulthood filled with possibilities to explore his giftedness . . . or not. Either way, the choice is his.

The last "on the other hand . . . " issue I wish to raise involves living for the moment. As mentioned in a previous chapter, from the time gifted kids are little, those who care about them often address them in the future tense. Comments like "with your abilities, you can become anything you want to be when you grow up," or "someone with your brain will really be able to make a difference in the world" are inspiring comments to hear, yet they are laced with potential pitfalls. Not only are the children who absorb these compliments prone to wonder if their future choices will measure up to others' expectations, they may also question if the phase of life they are in now—childhood—is merely a means to a bigger end; a staging area for their "real lives" as adults. Thankfully, it's not. Consider this reality: We are grown-ups for about 80% of our lives. And, if you partial out the totally dependent years of infancy and pre-school, that leaves only about 12% of one's life to be a kid—to be innocent of and unencumbered by adult-size worries. Yet, with many gifted children, even that smidgen of time is violated. First, their own active minds are naturally going to seek the bigger picture and the higher truths. With large vocabularies in hand, they will seek answers to questions that even we, as adults, struggle to decipher. With each question, another chip is chunked away from their childhoods.

> Acknowledge their insights and global awareness of issues, and then go out and have a snowball fight, toss a Frisbee with them and the dog, build a house out of playing cards, or splash each other with mud so thick that you have to hose down outside.

What to do? Acknowledge their insights and global awareness of issues, and then go out and have a snowball fight, toss a Frisbee with them and the dog, build a house out of playing cards, or splash each other with mud so thick that you have to hose down outside. Because, as John Ross, valedictorian of his Ohio high school several years ago reminded his fellow graduates:

> Like countless people have asked countless other graduates, a man asked me, "What are you going to do with the rest of your life?"
>
> But as I stood there dumbfounded, eyebrows bent, mind perplexed, I realized I had no idea. And I realized, too, that it was good not to know and good not to have any idea.
>
> It was good not to know where my money will be invested in ten years or where I will be working in five. Good not to know for whom I wanted to work, or where, or why. It was good not to know how big my house will be or what car I'll drive. Good not to know about retirement or IRAs and 401K plans . . .

When you plan too much, you lose important things like watching cartoons and not caring that Wile E. Coyote comes back after every ill-timed attempt with boulders. Laughing at least 37 times every day. Loving everything and everybody because the world seems like one of those books that you save for a rainy day and a soft, high-backed chair by the window.

It was good not to know what I wanted to do, because when you're young and fresh and innocent, you can't go wrong. Someone once wrote, "When you're young, you're golden." So, wherever I go and whatever I do with the rest of my life, I'll always stay young and I'll always stay golden. (Delisle & Galbraith, 2002, p. 159)

John's view of life as a series of present-tense moments to be savored, laughed about, and enjoyed to their fullest is a refreshing reminder that even though the "best is yet to come" for our gifted children in future years, there is absolutely nothing wrong with relishing each new day with an aplomb that borders on giddiness. Can we, can our children, follow his lead?

Closing Time

For almost 25 years, I've been a professor of gifted child education at Kent State University. Most of my graduate students are teachers already—parents, too—and they are reentering higher education to earn the professional credential that allows them to teach in a gifted program in Ohio's public schools. It's been a remarkable journey for me to learn from them, and I can only hope that the reverse is true, as well.

Inevitably, when I teach the introductory course "Social and Emotional Components of Giftedness," I have a series of stragglers who stay after class to ask "a quick question" (. . . there is no such thing!), or to volunteer an admission that makes many of them feel uncomfortable. The conversations often go something like this:

"I'm really enjoying this course, Dr. Delisle," they begin.

"How so?" I ask.

"Well" (and this is where they often begin to squirm a bit), "when I signed up for the course, I figured I'd learn something about gifted children that I could take back and use in my classroom."

" . . . and is that happening?" I ask with anticipation.

More squirming. "Yes, it is," (followed by an extended pause).

"But, something else is happening, too," I offer.

Now, the floodgates open. Students, often with tear-filled eyes, explain how the course content—the discussion of overexcitabilities, the work of Roeper and Hollingworth, the words of gifted children discussing their own thoughts and beliefs—has caused them to come to a conclusion that they had ignored or disregarded for years: that they, or someone close to them at home, are gifted. Often, this realization comes with a mixture of joy, pain, sadness, and humility, ending in a statement that is not far from this one, " . . . and all this time, I thought I/my spouse/my daughter was just weird."

This oft-repeated scenario is a cathartic moment for an adult coming to grips with his or her own giftedness, or the giftedness of a loved one who has, heretofore, been misunderstood, dismissed, or looked at oddly by others. Frequently, from that moment on, these students begin opening up more in class, talking of personal experiences in school or life situations that cause head nods from many of their classmates, and asking questions that have been brewing in their minds for years.

Recently, one of my students, Laurel K. Chehayl, took these self-revelations to a higher plain, composing a poetic tribute to her son, and to herself. In doing so, she relates what graduate students, parents, and gifted children themselves have been sharing with me throughout my career—the desire to be understood and accepted as the gifted individuals that they are.

Reflection
By Laurel K. Chehayl

I have learned . . .

I'm not the only one
who feels stupid
being smart;
there may be a reason
my boy and I are feeling people—we cry
at movies, in museums,
upon reaching the ends of books.

I have learned . . .

I've not always made the best decisions
and wish I had more strength sometimes.
But I've learned, too, that my own—
and it's OK to use the word—
giftedness
has been a gift to him, to my motherhood
as I navigate with him the pain of
being told we're not living up to our
potential,

not remembering when we learned to read,
or being the only one, at 10,
with a deep passion for all things beautiful.

I have learned . . .

I've not always been the best teacher,
but I have been the best I can
and I've learned, now, because my eyes,
opening for the first time.
see who we
are, and those
that remind me of me, or him
are the ones that are like us
The gifted—
to be acknowledged, to be celebrated,
to hold up to the light in my heart,
examined and cherished.

But most importantly
I have learned
it's OK to say the word
. . . gifted.

(Chehayl, 2004, p. 4)

As this book ends, I have to wonder how many of the adults reading it came to it seeking answers for how to raise their own gifted children; how to understand them fully (or, at least, better); how to put into focus the radical differences in their levels of development across their intellectual, emotional, physical, and social realms; and how to convince others that having a gifted child is not as easy as it might seem. Yet, if you are like so many of my graduate students, I would bet a tidy sum that your reading has caused you the introspection Laurel discovered as she read about topics and issues that sounded very familiar; for in learning about your gifted child, some of you may have underlined passages that referred as much to you as they did to that gifted 12-year-old you've cuddled since birth. If so, welcome to the world of self-discovery!

Life is not a race to see who can get to the end the fastest. Taking each day as it comes, seeing each triumph and disappointment as simply stepping-stones to all the tomorrows that lie ahead, is a lesson you can teach your gifted kids every morning as they awake. A new day, a fresh perspective, another reason to shine: You have within you the power to help your gifted children appreciate themselves as the competent, caring young people you have come to cherish.

Enjoy the ride!

> Life is not a race to see who can get to the end the fastest. Taking each day as it comes, seeing triumph and disappointment as simply stepping-stones to all the tomorrows that lie ahead, is a lesson you can teach your gifted kids every morning as they awake . . .

Gifted Children Give Thanks

"For the most part, my relationship with my parents is an extremely warm and close one. They are extremely concerned with understanding me and being sympathetic to my needs (whether they be intellectual or emotional). They strongly desire that I be a person independent of themselves, and they acknowledge that my expectations, goals and beliefs are often different from theirs." (American Association for Gifted Children, 1978, p. 49).

"My family makes me so happy at home because they support me in things that other people say are stupid or boring. They can solve my problems with me and help me to get through my childhood easier. My family is always there and I can talk to them about anything and feel comfortable."

—Boy, age 14

Kids and Kites
By Robert J., age 11

Kites fly but they need an anchor
Kids roam but they need a home

If a kite loses its anchor, it falls
If a child loses his home, he declines

As a kite goes higher and higher
You give it more string
As a child grows older and older
You give him more freedom
But here the similarity ends
For kites (even with the most string imaginable)
Crash sooner or later
But kids
(if they are old enough)
Adjust safely and create new homes.

References

American Association for Gifted Children. (1978). *On being gifted*. New York: Walker.

Assouline, S., Colangelo, N., Lupkowski-Shoplik, A., & Forstadt, T. (2003). *Iowa Acceleration Scale* (2nd ed.). Scottsdale, AZ: Great Potential Press.

Boomer, L. (Creator/Executive producer). (2000). *Malcolm in the middle* [Television series]. Los Angeles: Fox Broadcasting Company.

Chehayl, L. (2004). Reflection. *Gifted Education Communicator, 35*(4), 4.

Colangelo, N., Assouline, S. G., & Gross, M. U. M. (2004). *A nation deceived: How schools hold back America's brightest students* (Vol. 1). Iowa City, IA: The Connie Belin & Jacqueline N. Blank International Center for Gifted Education and Talent Development.

Conley, D. (2000). *Honky*. Berkeley, CA: University of California Press.

Delisle, J. R. (2000). *Once upon a mind: The stories and scholars of gifted child education*. Fort Worth, TX: Harcourt Brace.

Delisle, J., & Galbraith, J. (2002). *When gifted kids don't have all the answers.* Minneapolis, MN: Free Spirit.

Delisle, J., & Lewis, B. A. (2003). *The survival guide for teachers of gifted kids.* Minneapolis, MN: Free Spirit.

Galbraith, J., & Delisle, J. (1996). *The gifted kids' survival guide: A teen handbook.* Minneapolis, MN: Free Spirit.

Gallagher, J., & Gallagher, S. (1994). *Teaching the gifted child* (4th ed.). Boston: Allyn & Bacon.

Goleman, D. (1995). *Emotional intelligence.* New York: Bantam.

Gurian, A. (2001). *Many gifted girls, few eminent women: Why?* Retrieved October 20, 2005, from http://aboutourkids.org/aboutour/articles/giftedgirls.html

Hollingworth, L. S. (1942). *Children above 180 IQ, Stanford-Binet: Origin and development.* Yonkers-on-Hudson, NY: World Book Company.

Kendrick, C. (2001, November). High achievers: What price do they pay? *ASCA School Counselor, 40.*

LaCoste-Caputto, J. (2005, February 19). They aren't going to take it anymore. *San Antonio Express News,* p. 8A.

Least Restrictive Environment (LRE) Coalition (2005). *What is LRE?* Retrieved October 20, 2005, from http://www.lrecoalition.org/01_WhatIsLRE

Lind, S. (2001). Overexcitability and the gifted. *SENG Newsletter, 1*(1), 3–6.

Phillips, C. (2001). *The philosophers' club.* Berkeley, CA: Tricycle Press.

Piechowski, M. M. (1991). Emotional development and emotional giftedness. In N. Colangelo & G. A. Davis (Eds.), *Handbook of gifted education* (pp. 285–306). Boston: Allyn & Bacon.

Piechowski, M. M., & Cunningham, K. (1985). Patterns of overexcitability in a group of artists. *Journal of Creative Behavior, 19,* 153–174.

Roeper, A. (1995). Gifted adults: Their characteristics and emotions. In *Annemarie Roeper: Selected writings and speeches* (pp. 93–108). Minneapolis, MN: Free Spirit.

Roeper, A. (2000). Giftedness is heart and soul. *Gifted Education Communicator, 31*(4), 32–33, 56–58.

Roeper, A. (2004). The qualitative assessment model. *Roeper Review, 26,* 33.

Rogers, K. (2002). *Re-forming gifted education.* Scottsdale, AZ: Great Potential Press.

Silverman, L. (1999, January). Parenting gifted children. *Parenting Network Newsletter,* 3–4.

Streznewski, M. K. (1999). *Gifted grownups: The mixed blessings of extraordinary potential.* New York: John Wiley.

Teen People staff. (2005, April). 20 teens who will change the world. *Teen People,* 104–114.

Torrance, E. P., Murdock, M., & Fletcher, D. C. (1996). *Creative problem solving through role playing.* Pretoria, Republic of South Africa: Benedic Books.

Veis, G. (2005, June). Finding the path. *GQ,* 166–168.

Walker, J. (Producer), & Bird, B. (Writer/Director). (2004). *The Incredibles* [Motion picture]. United States: Disney/Pixar.

Webb, J. T., Meckstroth, E. A., & Tolan, S. S. (1982). *Guiding the gifted child.* Scottsdale, AZ: Great Potential Press.

Webb, J. T., Amend, E. R., Webb, N. E., Goerss, J., Beljan, P., & Olenchak, F. R. (2005). *Misdiagnosis and dual diagnoses of gifted children and adults.* Scottsdale, AZ: Great Potential Press.

White, D. (2001). *Philosophy for kids.* Waco, TX: Prufrock Press.

Williamson, M. (1992). *A return to love: Reflections on the principles of "A course of miracles."* New York: HarperCollins.

Resources
for Parents
of Gifted Kids

Gifted Education Journals and Publications

Gifted Child Quarterly
Paula Olszewski-Kubilius, Editor
Northwestern University
617 Dartmouth Pl.
Evanston, IL 60208-4175
Phone: (847) 491-3782
Fax: (847) 467-4283
Web site: http://www.nagc.org

Gifted Child Today
Susan Johnsen, Editor
Baylor University
One Bear Place #97304
Waco, TX 76798-7304
Phone: (254) 710-6116

Web site: http://www.prufrock.com/client/client_pages/
prufrockjournalsmagazines.cfm

Gifted Education Communicator
Margaret Gosfield, Editor
15141 E. Whittier Blvd., Ste. 510
Whittier, CA 90603
Phone: (562) 789-9933
Web site: http://CAGifted.org

Gifted and Talented International
Joyce VanTassel-Baska, Editor
College of William and Mary
P.O. Box 8795
Williamsburg, VA 23187-8795
Phone: (757) 221-2185
Fax: (757) 221-2184
Web site: http://www.worldgifted.org/xpubs.htm

Journal for the Education of the Gifted
Tracy L. Cross, Editor
Indiana Academy, Ball State University
Muncie, IN 47306
Phone: (765) 285-7457
Fax: (765) 285-2777
Web site: http://www.prufrock.com/client/client_pages/
prufrockjournalsmagazines.cfm

Journal of Secondary Gifted Education
Bonnie Cramond, Editor
University of Georgia
323 Aderhold Hall
Athens, GA 30602-7143
Phone: (706) 542-4248

Web site: http://www.prufrock.com/client/client_pages/
prufrock_jm_jsge.cfm

Parenting for High Potential
Don Treffinger, Editor
Center for Creative Learning
P.O. Box 14100, NE Plaza
Sarasota, FL 34278-4100
Phone: (941) 342-9928
Fax: (941) 342-0064
Web site: http://www.nagc.org

Roeper Review
Don Ambrose, Editor
Graduate Department, School of Education
College of Liberal Arts, Education, and Sciences
Rider University
2083 Lawrenceville Rd.
Lawrenceville, NJ 08648-3099
Phone: (609) 895-5647
Fax: (215) 493-4945
Web site: http://www.roeperreview.org

Understanding Our Gifted
Dorothy Knopper, Publisher
Open Space Communications
P.O. Box 18268
Boulder, CO 80308
Phone: (303) 444-7020
Fax: (303) 545-6505
Web site: http://www.openspacecomm.com

United States National Gifted Associations and Department of Education

American Association for Gifted Children (AAGC)
Margaret Evans Gayle, Executive Director
Duke University
P.O. Box 90270
Durham, NC 27708-0270
Phone: (919) 783-6152
E-mail: megayle@aol.com
Web site: http://www.aagc.org

Council for Exceptional Children (CEC)
1110 N. Glebe Rd., Suite 300
Arlington, VA 22201-5704
Phone: (888) 232-7733; (703) 620-3660
Fax: (703) 264-9494
E-mail: service@cec.sped.org
Web site: http://www.cec.sped.org

The Association for the Gifted (TAG)
Diane Montgomery
Oklahoma State University
424 Willard Hall
Stillwater, OK 74078-3031
Phone: (405) 744-9441
Fax: (405) 744-6756
E-mail: montgom@okstate.edu
Web site: http://www.cectag.org

National Association for Gifted Children (NAGC)
1701 L St. NW, Ste. 550
Washington, DC 20036
Phone: (202) 785-4268

Fax: (202) 785-4248
E-mail: nagc@nagc.org
Web site: http://www.nagc.org

The National Foundation for Gifted and Creative Children (NFGCC)
395 Diamond Hill Road
Warwick, RI 02886-8554
Phone: (401) 738-0937
Web site: http://www.nfgcc.org

Supporting the Emotional Needs of the Gifted (SENG)
P.O. Box 6074
Scottsdale, AZ 85261
Phone: (773) 907-8092
E-mail: office@sengifted.org
Web site: http://www.sengifted.org

U.S. Department of Education
400 Maryland Ave. SW
Washington, DC 20202-0498
Phone: (800) 872-5327
Fax: (202) 401-0689
Web site: http://www.ed.gov

Centers for Gifted Education

Center for Creative Learning
Don Treffinger, President
P.O. Box 14100, NE Plaza
Sarasota, FL 34278-4100
Phone: (941) 342-9928
Fax: (941) 342-0064
E-mail: info@creativelearning.com
Web site: http://www.creativelearning.com

The Center for Gifted
Joan Franklin Smutny, Director
National-Louis University
P.O. Box 364
Wilmette, IL 60091
Phone: (847) 905-2150
E-mail: jrinne@nl.edu
Web site: http://www.thecenterforgifted.com

Center for Gifted Education
Ann Robinson
University of Arkansas at Little Rock
Gifted Programs
2801 S. University Ave.
Little Rock, AR 72204
Phone: (501)569-3401
E-mail: aerobinson@ualr.edu
Web site: http://giftedctr.ualr.edu

Center for Gifted Education
Sally Dobyns, Director
University of Louisiana–Lafayette
P.O. Box 44872
Lafayette, LA 70504-4872

Phone: (337) 482-6678
Fax: (337) 482-5842
E-mail: sdobyns@louisiana.edu
Web site: http://www.coe.louisiana.edu/centers/gifted.html

Center for Gifted Education
Margo Long, Director
Whitworth College
300 W. Hawthorne Road
Spokane, WA 99251
Phone: (509) 777-3226
E-mail: gifted@whitworth.edu.
Web site: http://www.whitworth.
edu/Academic/Department/Education/Gifted

The Center for Gifted Education
Joyce VanTassel-Baska, Executive Director
College of William and Mary
P.O. Box 8795
Williamsburg, VA 23187-8795
Phone: (757) 221-2362
Fax: (757) 221-2184
E-mail: cfge@wm.edu
Web site: http://www.cfge.wm.edu

The Center for Gifted Studies
Julia Roberts, Director
Western Kentucky University
1906 College Heights Blvd. #71031
Bowling Green, KY 42101-1031
Phone: (270) 745-6323
Fax: (270) 745-6279
E-mail: gifted@wku.edu
Web site: http://www.wku.edu/gifted

Center for Gifted Studies and Talent Development
Cheryll M. Adams, Director
Ball State University
Burris School 109
Muncie, IN 47306
Phone: (765) 285-5390
Fax: (765) 285-5455
E-mail: cadams@bsu.edu
Web site: http://www.bsu.edu/gifted

Center for Talent Development
Paula Olszewski-Kubilius, Director
School of Education and Social Policy
Northwestern University
617 Dartmouth Pl.
Evanston, IL 60208-4175
Phone: (847) 491-3782
Fax: (847) 467-4283
E-mail: ctd@northwestern.edu
Web site: http://www.ctd.northwestern.edu

Center for Talented Youth (CTY)
Lea Ybarra, Executive Director
Johns Hopkins University
McAuley Hall
5801 Smith Ave., Ste. 400
Baltimore, MD 21209
Phone: (410) 735-4100
Fax: (410) 735-6200
E-mail: ctyinfo@jhu.edu
Web site: http://www.jhu.edu/gifted

Centre for Gifted Education
University of Calgary
170 Education Block
2500 University Dr. NW
Calgary, Alberta, Canada T2N 1N4
Phone: (403) 220-7799
Fax: (403) 210-2068
E-mail: gifteduc@ucalgary.ca
Web site: http://www.ucalgary.ca/~gifteduc

DISCOVER Projects
C. June Maker
Department of Special Education
Rehabilitation & School Psychology
College of Education
University of Arizona
Tucson, AZ 85721-0069
Phone: (520) 622-8106
Fax: (520) 621-3821
E-mail: discover@email.arizona.edu
Web site: http://discover.arizona.edu

Drury University Center for Gifted Education
Marry Potthof, Pre-College Coordinator
Drury University
900 N. Benton Ave.
Springfield, MO 65802
Phone: (800) 922-2274
E-mail: mpotthof@drury.edu
Web site: http://www.drury.edu/section/section.
cfm?sid=150

Duke University Talent Identification Program (TIP)
P.O. Box 90780
Durham, NC 27708-0780
Phone: (919) 668-9100
Fax: (919) 681-7921
E-mail: information@tip.duke.edu
Web site: http://www.tip.duke.edu

The Frances A. Karnes Center for Gifted Studies
Frances A. Karnes, Director
University of Southern Mississippi
P.O. Box 8207
Hattiesburg, MS 39406-8207
Phone: (601) 266-5236
Fax: (601) 266-4978
E-mail: Gifted.Studies@usm.edu
Web site: http://www.usm.edu/~gifted

Gifted Development Center
Linda Kreger Silverman
1452 Marion St.
Denver, CO 80218
Phone: (303) 837-8378
Fax: (303) 831-7465
E-mail: gifted@gifteddevelopment.com
Web site: http://www.gifteddevelopment.com

Gifted Education Resource Institute (GERI)
Sidney M. Moon, Director
Purdue University
Beering Hall, Rm. 5113
100 N. University St.
West Lafayette, IN 47907-2098

Phone: (765) 494-7243
Fax: (765) 496-2706
E-mail: geri@purdue.edu
Web site: http://www.geri.soe.purdue.edu

Leta Hollingworth Center for the Study and Education of the Gifted

James Borland and Lisa R. Wright, Directors
Teachers College, Columbia University
TC Box 170
309 Main Hall, 525 W. 120th St.
New York, NY 10027
Phone: (212) 678-3851
E-mail: hollingworth@exchange.tc.columbia.edu
Web site: http://www.tc.columbia.edu/centers/hollingworth

National Research Center on the Gifted and Talented (NRC/GT)

Carolyn Callahan, Director
University of Virginia
Curry School of Education
P.O. Box 400277
Charlottesville, VA 22904-4277
Phone: (804) 924-4557
Fax: (804) 982-2383
E-mail: NRCGT@virginia.edu
Web site: http://curry.edschool.virginia.edu/go/NRC

Neag Center for Gifted Education and Talent Development

University of Connecticut
2131 Hillside Road, Unit 3007
Storrs, CT 06269-3007
Phone: (860) 486-4826

Fax: (860) 486-2900
Web site: http://www.gifted.uconn.edu

Torrance Center for Creativity and Talent Development
Department of Educational Psychology
323 Aderhold Hall
University of Georgia
Athens, GA 30602-7146
Phone: (706) 542-5104
Fax: (706) 542-4659
E-mail: creative@uga.edu
Web site: http://www.coe.uga.edu/Torrance

Web sites:

National Association for Gifted Children
http://www.nagc.org

A Nation Deceived
http://nationdeceived.org

Hoagie's Gifted Page
http://www.hoagiesgifted.org

GT World
http://www.gtworld.org

ERIC Clearinghouse on Disabilities and Gifted Education
http://www.ericec.org

Davidson Institute for Talent Development
http://www.ditd.org

State Associations and Departments of Education Web sites

Alabama Association for Gifted Children (AAGC)
http://aagc.freeservers.com/aagc.html

Alaska Department of Education and Early Development
http://www.eed.state.ak.us

Arizona Association for Gifted and Talented
http://www.azagt.org

Arizona Department of Education, Office of Gifted Education
http://www.ade.state.az.us/ess/gifted

Arkansas Department of Education
http://arkedu.state.ar.us

California Association for the Gifted (CAG)
http://www.cagifted.org

California Department of Education, Gifted and Talented Education (GATE)
http://www.cde.ca/gov/sp/gt

Colorado Association for Gifted and Talented
http://www.coloradogifted.org

Colorado Department of Education, Gifted and Talented Services
http://www.cde.state.co.us/index_special.htm

Connecticut Association for the Gifted (CAG)
http://www.CTGifted.org

Connecticut State Department of Education, Gifted and Talented
http://www.state.ct.us/sde/dtl/curriculum/currgift.htm

Delaware Department of Education
http://www.doe.state.de.us

District of Columbia State Education Office
http://seo.dc.gov

Florida Association for the Gifted (FLAG)
http://www.flagifted.org

Florida Gifted Network
http://www.floridagiftednet.org

Georgia Association for Gifted Children
http://www.gagc.org

Hawaii Department of Education/Gifted Education
http://www.k12.hi.us/~gtstate

Idaho–The Association for Gifted/State Advocates for Gifted Education (ITAG/SAGE)
http://www.itag-sage.org

Idaho State Department of Education, Gifted and Talented
http://www.sde.state.id.us/GiftedTalented

Illinois Association for Gifted Children
http://www.iagcgifted.org

Indiana Association for the Gifted (IAG)
http://www.iag-online.org

**Indiana Department of Education,
Gifted and Talented Education**
http://ideanet.doe.state.in.us/exceptional/gt

Iowa Talented and Gifted Association (ITAG)
http://iowatag.org

**Kansas Association for the Gifted, Talented, and
Creative**
http://www.kgtc.org

Kentucky Association for Gifted Education (KAGE)
http://www.wku.edu/kage

**Louisiana Department of Education Division
of Special Populations**
http://www.doe.state.la.us/lde

Maine Department of Education
Web site: http://www.state.me.us/education/homepage.
htm

**Gifted and Talented Association
of Montgomery County, Maryland**
http://www.groups.yahoo.com/group1GTAletters

Maryland Department of Education
http://www.marylandpublicschools.org/msde

Massachusetts Association for Gifted Education (MAGE)
http://www.MASSGifted.org

Michigan Alliance for Gifted Education (MAGE)
http://www.migiftedchild.org

Minnesota Council for the Gifted and Talented
http://www.MCGT.net

Mississippi Department of Education (Gifted Education)
http://www.mde.k12.ms.us/ACAD/ID/Curriculum/
Gifted/gifted.html

Gifted Association of Missouri (GAM)
http://www.mogam.org

Missouri Department of Elementary and Secondary Education, Gifted Education Programs
http://www.dese.state.mo.us/divimprove/gifted

Montana Association of Gifted and Talented Education
http://www.mtagate.org

Nebraska Association for the Gifted
http://www.NebraskaGifted.org

Nevada Association for Gifted and Talented (NAGT)
http://www.nevadagt.org

New Hampshire Association for Gifted Education (NHAGE)
http://www.nhage.org

New Jersey Association for Gifted Children (NJAGC)
http://www.njagc.org

New Mexico State Department of Education
http://www.sde.state.nm.us

Advocacy for Gifted and Talented Education in New York (AGATE)
http://www.agateny.org

North Carolina Association for the Gifted and Talented (NCAGT)
http://www.ncagt.org

North Carolina State Board of Education, Exceptional Children Division
http://www.ncpublicschools.org/ec

North Dakota Department of Public Instruction
http://www.dpi.state.nd.us

Ohio Association for Gifted Children (OAGC)
http://www.oagc.com

Ohio Department of Education, Office for Exceptional Children
http://www.ode.state.oh.us/exceptional_children/Gifted_Children

Oklahoma Association for Gifted, Creative, and Talented (OAGCT)
http://www.oagct.org

Oklahoma State Department of Education, Gifted and Talented Office
http://title3.sde.state.ok.us/gifted

Oregon Association for Talented and Gifted (OATAG)
http://www.oatag.org

Pennsylvania Association for Gifted Education (PAGE)
http://www.penngifted.org

Pennsylvania Department of Education, Gifted Education
http://www.pde.state.pa.us/gifted_ed

Rhode Island Advocates for Gifted Education (RIAGE)
http://www.riage.org

Rhode Island Department of Elementary and Secondary Education, Special Education Talent Development
http://www.ridoe.net/Special_needs/talentdev.htm

South Carolina Department of Education, Gifted and Talented
http://www.myscschools.com/offices/cso/Gifted_Talented/gt.htm

South Dakota Association for Gifted Education
Web site: http://www.sd-agc.org

Tennessee Association for the Gifted (TAG)
http://www.tag-tenn.org

Texas Association for the Gifted and Talented (TAGT)
http://www.txgifted.org

Texas Education Agency,
Division of Advanced Academic Services
http://www.tea.state.tx.us/gted

Utah Association for Gifted Children (UAGC)
http://www.uagc.org

Utah State Office of Education, Gifted and Talented
http://www.usoe.k12.ut.us/curr/gift_talent

Vermont Council for Gifted Education
http://www.vcge.org

Virginia Association for the Gifted
http://www.vagifted.org

Virginia Department of Education,
Gifted Education
http://www.pen.k12.va.us/VDOE/Instruction/Gifted/
gifted.htm

Washington Association of Educators
of the Talented and Gifted (WAETG)
http://www.waetag.net

West Virginia Association for Gifted and Talented (WVAGT)
http://www.geocities.com/wvgifted

West Virginia Department of Education, Office of Special Education
http://wvde.state.wv.us/ose

Wisconsin Association for Gifted and Talented (WATG)
http://www.focol.org/watg

Wisconsin Department of Public Instruction, Gifted and Talented
http://www.dpi.wi.gov/dae

Wyoming State Department of Education
http://www.k12.wy.us

Canadian Gifted Education Resources

Gifted Canada
http://www3.bc.sympatico.ca/giftedcanada

Canadian Council for Exceptional Children
http://canadian.cec.sped.org

Centre for Gifted Education
University of Calgary
http://www.ucalgary.ca/~gifteduc

Alberta Associations for Bright Children (AABC/ Alberta)
http://www.planet.eon.net/~tomcejra/aabc

Gifted Children's Association of British Columbia
http://www.gcabc.ca

Manitoba Education and Youth
http://www.edu.gov.mb.ca

The Association for Bright Children,
New Brunswick Chapter
http://www.sjfn.nb.ca/community_hall/A/asso4180.html

Newfoundland and Labrador Association
for Gifted Children (NLAGC)
http://www.cdli.ca/nlagc/nlagc.html

Association for Bright Children of Nova Scotia
http://atlanticsciencelinks.dal.ca/stanet/database/abc.html

Ontario Association for Bright Children
http://www.abcontario.ca

Ontario Gifted
http://www.ontariogifted.org

Prince Edward Island Department of Education
http://www.edu.pe.ca

Ministère de l'Éducation/Education Québec
http://www.meq.gouv.qc.ca/GR-PUB/m_englis.htm

Saskatchewan Learning
http://www.sasked.gov.sk.ca

Saskatchewan Teachers' Federation Gifted Resources
http://www.stf.sk.ca/src/prof_res_serv/bibliog/gifted.htm

Government of the Northwest Territories: Education, Culture, and Employment
http://www.ece.gov.nt.ca

Nunavik Department of Education
http://www.gov.nu.ca/Nunavut/English/phone/education.shtml

Government of Yukon: Department of Education
http://www.gov.yk.ca/services/departments/education.html

About the Author

Jim Delisle has been involved in gifted child education for 30 years, as a teacher, counselor, college professor, and parent. Jim's academic career has been spent at Kent State University in Ohio, and his public school experiences have included teaching children with learning and behavioral difficulties, teaching fourth grade, and teaching gifted children in middle and high school settings.

An avid writer, Jim has published 14 books and more than 200 articles. Never afraid to question longstanding orthodoxies, Jim speaks out on controversial issues that affect gifted children's lives. These stances, often unpopular among his colleagues, leave him with fewer friends, but deeper friendships.

Upon retirement, Jim plans to teach writing in a juvenile detention facility and to write children's books featuring kids whose lives have enveloped his own. He and his wife, Deb, plan to relocate to a warm state with an ocean view.